VALUES IN ACTION ®
Twenty Real Life Stories

COURAGE

By
Kathleen J. Edgar
Susan E. Edgar
and
Joanne Mattern

Reading CHALLENGE®

PHOTO CREDITS

AP/Wide World: pp. 21, 43, 76, 90, 98, 123 • **Corbis/Bettmann:** p. 66 • **Library of Congress, Prints and Photography Division:** pp. 19, 113 • **The Granger Collection:** pp. 39, 55, 83, 94, 107

www.readingchallenge.com

a division of
Learning Challenge, Inc.
569 Boylston Street
Boston, MA 02116

Copyright © 2004 Learning Challenge, Inc.

All rights reserved including the right of
reproduction in whole or in part in any form.

Manufactured in the United States of America

0404-1MV

Library of Congress Cataloging-in-Publication Data

Edgar, Kathleen J.
Courage / by Kathy Edgar, Susan Edgar, Joanne Mattern.
p. cm. -- (Values in action, twenty real life stories)
Summary: Twenty short biographies of men and women whose lives and work embody the value of courage.
Includes bibliographical references and index.
ISBN 1-59203-056-4 (hardcover)
1. Biography—Juvenile literature. 2. Courage—Juvenile literature. 3. Values—Juvenile literature. [1. Courage. 2. Biography.] I. Edgar, Susan E. II. Mattern, Joanne, 1963- III. Title.
CT107.E34 2003   920.02—dc22
                    2003013728

Reading CHALLENGE®

Dear Parents and Educators:

Reading Challenge® is pleased to introduce a new Literacy and Character Education program— **Values in Action® Twenty Real Life Stories.**

These twenty fascinating biographies are perfect for classroom study, homeschooling, and supplemental reading. The stories foster an appreciation of important values that form the basis of sound character education.

Each real life story comes to life with a time line and quotes. In addition, each book contains a value-discussion section, a glossary and pronunciation guide, and an index. These elements give readers the tools they need to fully appreciate the inspiring biographies within.

"Open a book . . . and the world opens to you."

The Editors
Reading Challenge

A division of Learning Challenge, Inc.
www.learningchallenge.com

Contents

Courage in Action 5
Neil Armstrong: *First Person on the Moon*. 7
James Bowie: *Hero of the Frontier* 13
Benjamin O. Davis Jr.: *A Very Special Soldier* 18
David Farragut: *Fearless Commander* 25
Geronimo: *Apache Warrior* 31
Nathan Hale: *Only One Life to Give* 37
Fannie Lou Hamer: *Fighting for Freedom* 42
Wild Bill Hickok: *Lawman of the Wild West* 48
Anne Hutchinson: *Champion of Religious Freedom* . . 54
Andrew Jackson: *President of the Common People* . . . 60
Joan of Arc: *Military Hero, Martyr, Saint*. 65
Francis Marion: *The Swamp Fox* 70
John McCain: *Bravery Under Pressure* 75
Eddie Rickenbacker: *Flying Ace* 81
Sally Ride: *First American Woman in Space* 87
Sacagawea: *Guide to the West*. 93
Robert Smalls: *An Unlikely Hero* 100
Mary Edwards Walker: *Army Doctor* 106
Ida B. Wells-Barnett: *Antilynching Activist* 112
Chuck Yeager: *Breaking the Sound Barrier* 118
Glossary and Pronunciation Guide 125
Index 127

Courage in Action

How the Lives of 20 Remarkable People Illustrate the Value of Courage

Courage is the ability to face and overcome a fear. A courageous person may feel scared, but does not let that feeling get in the way of accomplishing something. A firefighter shows courage every time he or she enters a burning building. A sick person shows courage when he or she undergoes an operation. Men and women in the military show courage under fire during combat. Courage comes in all shapes and sizes, from braving the first day at a new school to facing an illness or the death of a loved one.

You have probably shown courage at times in your life. Have you ever been nervous about giving a report in class? If so, you were courageous when you stood up in front of all those people and gave your report, even though you were scared to do so. Perhaps you stood up to a bully at school, or rode a bike without training wheels for the first time. Any time that you face a frightening challenge, you show courage.

There have been many people throughout history who have displayed remarkable courage. Neil Armstrong, an astronaut who faced more than a

Courage

few scary experiences in space, is one example. He continued to explore space even though it was dangerous. Eventually, he became the first human to set foot on the moon.

Ida B. Wells-Barnett was a civil-rights activist who lived during a time of great discrimination. Even though her life was threatened, Wells-Barnett spoke out boldly to protest violence against African Americans. She risked her own life to help better the lives of others. She did not let the fear of what might happen to her get in the way of her work.

The courage of Nathan Hale is another inspiration. He was a young man who fought the British during the American Revolution. He agreed to spy on the enemy to find out when they might attack. This was a very dangerous job, but Hale insisted on doing it. He knew that it would help the American army. Eventually, he was captured and killed, but his bravery made him one of America's most famous heroes.

The people in this book accomplished wonderful things because of their courage. Sometimes it might seem very hard to be courageous. But that is what true courage is: doing the harder but better thing. Being courageous means accepting and taking on a challenge. That is something that anyone can do.

Neil Armstrong
First Person on the Moon
(born 1930)

During the 1960s, President John F. Kennedy set a challenging goal for the U.S. space program: to put a man on the moon by the end of the decade. The U.S. achieved that goal, and astronaut Neil Armstrong became the first person in history to walk on the moon.

Born to Fly

Neil Alden Armstrong was born on August 5, 1930, in Wapakoneta, Ohio. When he was six years old, he took his first flight in a small airplane. From that day on, all he wanted to do was fly.

Neil Armstrong started learning to fly when he was 14 years old. He worked at a local drugstore for less than 50 cents an hour to pay for his lessons. At 16, he got his pilot's license. He did not even have his driver's license yet, but he could fly a plane!

Armstrong went to college at Purdue University in Indiana. There, he joined the Naval Air Cadet program. Two years later, he was called into active duty in the Navy. Sent to fight in the Korean War, he saw action in several battles and was awarded three Air Medals for his bravery. After he finished his Navy service, Armstrong went back to college. When he graduated in 1955, he got a job as a test pilot for the U.S. government.

The Race for Space

In 1958, the U.S. government formed the National Aeronautics and Space Administration (NASA). NASA's goal was to send a man into outer space, and eventually put a man on the moon.

When Neil Armstrong heard about the new space program, he and 200 other people applied to join. In September 1962, Armstrong received the good news that he—along with just eight other men—had been chosen for NASA's program, called Gemini.

Armstrong spent hundreds of hours training to be an astronaut. He learned to master the complicated instruments that made a spaceship fly. He studied physics, astronomy, and other sciences. He trained in machines that taught him what it felt like to fly in space.

On March 16, 1966, Armstrong and another astronaut, David Scott, flew a spaceship named *Gemini 8* into orbit.

> **"Tranquility base here; the *Eagle* has landed."**
>
> —Neil Armstrong to mission control as the *Eagle* touched down on the moon

*Astronaut Neil Armstrong poses in front
of a photograph of Earth's moon.*

◈ Courage ◈

Once in space, it was to dock with a satellite. The docking went fine, but afterward, *Gemini 8* began to tumble end over end. Nothing that the two astronauts tried could stop the ship from spinning. Finally, Armstrong took the controls and, after a 30-minute struggle, gained control of the ship. After *Gemini 8* landed, experts discovered that an electrical problem had been responsible for the tumbling. Everyone at NASA was amazed that Armstrong had figured out how to save the ship and get back to Earth safely.

Walking on the Moon

Then as now, space travel was dangerous. The goal of landing on the moon was especially so. In 1967, three astronauts training for the moon mis-

TOPICAL TIDBIT

The Father of Modern Rocketry

One of the hardest things about making the U.S. space program work was giving spacecraft enough power to fly thousands of miles from Earth. Robert H. Goddard figured out how to do it. In 1889, at age 17, he starting trying to build rockets whose dangerously explosive power could be controlled, making them safe enough to blast humans into space. He launched his first liquid-fuel rocket in 1926. By 1935, he had one that could travel faster than the speed of sound. Goddard died in 1945, but without his hard work, the *Apollo 11* crew could never have made the 1969 flight to the moon—about 239,000 miles from Earth.

◆ Neil Armstrong ◆

sion were killed while still on the launch pad: A fire had broken out aboard their *Apollo 1* spacecraft. Still, Armstrong and the other Apollo astronauts pressed on. Finally, on July 16, 1969, Neil Armstrong, Edwin "Buzz" Aldrin, and Michael Collins climbed into the *Apollo 11* spacecraft and blasted off toward the moon.

The journey to the moon took four days. On the morning of July 20, Collins remained in orbit in the *Columbia*. This was the command module of *Apollo 11*. Armstrong and Aldrin crawled into a smaller unit called the *Eagle* and set out for the surface of the moon.

As Armstrong and Aldrin approached the moon, they realized that the *Eagle* was about to crash into a large rock. Armstrong grabbed the controls and steered the *Eagle* to a safe landing.

LIFE EVENTS

1930
Neil Alden Armstrong is born in Wapakoneta, Ohio.

1955
Armstrong becomes a test pilot for the National Advisory Committee for Aeronautics, an agency that becomes NASA in 1958.

1962
Armstrong joins NASA's Gemini program.

1966
Armstrong commands the *Gemini 8* mission, performing the first docking of one spacecraft with another.

1969
Commanding the *Apollo 11* flight, Armstrong becomes the first person to walk on the moon.

Courage

Just a few hours later, Armstrong climbed out of the spaceship and became the first human being to set foot on the moon. As his feet touched the lunar surface, he said these now-famous words: "That's one small step for man, one giant leap for mankind."

Armstrong and Aldrin spent less than a day on the moon. They collected rocks and other specimens for scientists to study back on Earth. They also planted a U.S. flag on the moon's surface, along with a plaque that said:

> HERE MEN FROM THE PLANET EARTH
> FIRST SET FOOT UPON THE MOON
> JULY 1969 A.D.
> WE CAME IN PEACE FOR ALL MANKIND

Armstrong and Aldrin climbed back into the *Eagle* for the flight back to their command module, the *Columbia*, which was still orbiting overhead. Then they turned their spacecraft back toward Earth.

Four days later, the three *Apollo 11* astronauts splashed down safely in the Pacific Ocean.

After the Moon

Neil Armstrong worked at NASA until 1971, when he retired. Today, he lives a quieter life with his family in Ohio. He remains a model of courage to anyone who ever dreamed of reaching for the stars.

James Bowie
Hero of the Frontier
(born 1796 • died 1836)

Frontiersman James Bowie

Courage

In 1836, a group of courageous Texans tried to defend the Alamo from an attack by Mexican soldiers. One of the heroes of that battle was a man named James Bowie. Even before the Alamo, Bowie was well-known as one of the West's bravest adventurers.

A Wild Past

James Bowie was born in Kentucky on April 10, 1796. When James was six, his father, Rezin, decided that life in Tennessee had grown too settled and too crowded. He moved the family to Louisiana. James and his brothers learned how to hunt, fish, trap, plant crops, and tend herds of cattle. They became known as "those wild Bowie boys" because they were always looking for an adventure.

The Bowie Knife

In 1827, James Bowie was involved in a street fight in Alexandria, Louisiana. He used a large hunting knife to defend himself against three attackers. The fight was written up in newspapers, which described the knife's unusually long, thin blade. Bowie became famous as

> "Keep under cover, boys, and reserve your fire; we haven't a man to spare."
> —James Bowie

the "inventor of the Bowie knife." (Historians now believe that Rezin Jr., James's brother, actually came up with the knife's design.) The Bowie knife soon became a popular weapon in the U.S. and England.

On to Texas

By 1830, Bowie had moved to San Antonio, Texas, which was then part of Mexico. He became a Mexican citizen and married the daughter of one of San Antonio's most important men.

Bowie spent the next few years searching for lost Spanish silver mines and fighting Native Americans as a Texas Ranger. In 1833, his wife and children died of a disease called cholera. Bowie became even more restless and daring then. With his family gone, it seemed, he no longer cared what happened to him.

TOPICAL TIDBIT

Before Texas Was Texas

The first residents of the area now called Texas were a group of Indian tribes, including an alliance called the Caddo confederacies. Europeans arrived in mid 1519. In 1821, Texas became a part of Mexico. In 1823, Stephen F. Austin received a grant from Mexico to start his first colony of settlers along the lower Brazos and Colorado rivers.

◆ Courage ◆

Remember the Alamo!

In 1835, Texans began a war to win independence from Mexico. Mexico's president, Antonio López de Santa Anna, was planning to attack San Antonio. When Bowie heard of the plan, he offered to lead a group of volunteers to defend a storehouse at the Alamo. The Alamo was a former church that was being used as a fort. On January 19, 1836, Bowie and his 30 men joined Colonel James Neill and more than 75 soldiers at the Alamo. They soon found that most of the supplies were already gone. Bowie sent an urgent message to the Texas governor, asking for men, money, rifles, and cannon powder.

Before supplies could reach them, however, about 8,000 Mexican soldiers arrived. Bowie was sick with pneumonia. He also had a broken hip from a fall while mounting a cannon on one of the Alamo's walls. Davy Crockett, who was another hero of the frontier, was also at the Alamo. He wrote about how Colonel Bowie would crawl from his cot every day to show his support for the other men.

Bowie and his companions did their best to defend the fort. But they were hopelessly outnumbered. On March 6, 1836, the Mexican army stormed into the Alamo and killed all of the rebels.

◆ James Bowie ◆

LIFE EVENTS

1796
James Bowie is born in Logan County, Kentucky.

1827
The "Bowie knife"—a heavy knife with a long, thin blade—becomes famous after a street fight.

1830
Bowie moves to Texas, a province of Mexico.

1835
Texas starts a war of independence from Mexico. Bowie is a colonel in the Texas army.

1836
James Bowie dies in defense of the Alamo.

Never afraid to back down, James Bowie died as he had lived—courageously. He went down in history as one of America's bravest heroes and most colorful characters. ◆

Benjamin O. Davis Jr.
A Very Special Soldier
(born 1912 • died 2002)

Through much of the early 20th century, it was hard for African Americans to find opportunity in the U.S. military. During that time, Benjamin O. Davis Jr. overcame the odds and became one of the most powerful and respected men in military service.

A Military Family

Benjamin Oliver Davis Jr. was born on December 18, 1912, in Washington, D.C. His father, Benjamin O. Davis Sr., was the first black brigadier (one-star) general in the U.S. Army. The Davis family moved many times as Benjamin Sr. took on military assignments around the country. For a while, young Benjamin and his siblings lived with their grandparents while their father was serving in the Philippines.

Benjamin Jr. did well in school. A popular student, he was elected president of the student council. Afterward, he went on to attend Western Reserve University in Cleveland and the University of Chicago.

Captain Benjamin O. Davis Jr. climbs into an advanced trainer at the basic advanced flying school for Negro air corps cadets.

His father wanted him to enter the U.S. Military Academy at West Point. Benjamin did not know if he wanted a military career. At that time, West Point was not eager to have black students. Still, he took the entrance exam—and failed.

◇ Courage ◇

Benjamin Davis was shocked when he failed the exam. Suddenly, he wanted to prove to himself and to his father that he could succeed at the academy. He studied hard and passed the test on his second try. He entered West Point on July 1, 1932.

The Silent Treatment

Davis was not welcome at West Point. The other cadets did not want a black man in their class. For four years, they subjected him to "silencing." No one ate with him or would room with him. No cadets spoke to him unless absolutely necessary. This made Davis even more determined to succeed. In 1936, he graduated in the top 13 percent of his class. He was the first African American West Point graduate in the 20th century.

After graduating, Davis had a series of unimportant jobs. He and his new wife had to live in segregated military housing, which meant that they were separated from white families. Then, World War II began, and everything changed.

Blacks and Whites in the Army

When the U.S. entered World War II in 1941, the army was segregated. Black soldiers and white soldiers fought in separate units, commanded by officers of their own color. The highest-ranking officers, however, were white.

Because the U.S. Army needed pilots for the war, it started an Advanced Army Flying School for blacks at

Major General Davis in his Pentagon office in 1965 after President Lyndon Johnson nominated him for promotion to lieutenant general

Tuskegee Institute. Benjamin O. Davis Jr. was in its first class. In 1943, the Ninety-ninth Pursuit Squadron headed to North Africa under Davis's command. The squadron, known as the Tuskegee Airmen, flew many missions in a short time. Still, they struggled against discrimination. One white commander

◆ Courage ◆

said that the men of the Ninety-ninth did not have the same desire to fight as white pilots. A white general agreed, and it looked as if the Tuskegee Airmen were finished.

Davis returned to the U.S. to stick up for his men. He insisted to the War Department that the Ninety-ninth fought just as hard. He said it had in fact flown more missions than the white squadrons. The War Department was convinced by his arguments. In January 1944, it sent Davis and his Tuskegee Airmen to Europe to join the fight there.

Now part of the 332nd Fighter Group, the Tuskegee Airmen escorted bombers over Italy. Right away, they proved themselves in a series of fierce battles. In one two-week period, they shot down seven German fighters for every one they lost. Davis led the 332nd on its most spectacular mission, a 1,600-mile trip to Berlin.

> "Suddenly the air was full of P-47s [jets], diving and whirling through our formations. They never left us. They showed no inclination to turn away from the flak rising up ahead. They flew through the clouds of bursting shells. . . . It was a grand gesture."
>
> —a U.S. bomber pilot, describing the bravery of the Tuskegee Airmen fighting in Italy, 1943

Benjamin O. Davis Jr.

By the end of the war, the squadron had flown more than 200 escort missions, had shot down 111 enemy planes in the air, and had not lost a single bomber in their care. The Tuskegee Airmen had proven that they were just as brave and skilled as white pilots. Benjamin O. Davis Jr. received the Distinguished Flying Cross, which is a medal awarded to those who show extraordinary heroism and bravery during battle.

The war ended in 1945, but Davis found a new battle to fight: arguing for an end to segregation in the U.S. armed forces. In 1948, President Harry S. Truman signed an order ending segregation in the military. The 332nd Fighter Group became the first all-black unit to be integrated into the Air Force.

TOPICAL TIDBIT

Like Father, Like Son

As a groundbreaking military man, Benjamin O. Davis Jr. followed in the footsteps of his father. Benjamin O. Davis Sr. was born in 1877. He served during the Spanish-American War (1898) before being commissioned a second lieutenant in the Army in 1901— the first African American officer in the U.S. military. He later became the U.S. Army's first black colonel, then its first black general. But Davis Sr.'s career was limited by discrimination. It took the courage of his son to permanently open doors that had been closed to him and millions of other African Americans.

Away From the Spotlight

During the Korean War (1950-1953), Davis commanded an integrated flying unit. In 1959, he was promoted to major (two-star) general. He was the first African American to achieve such a high rank in the Air Force. In 1965, he became the first black lieutenant (three-star) general. During the late 1960s, he commanded the 13th Air Force in Vietnam. Then, in 1970, he retired.

Davis died on July 4, 2002. By then, the U.S. armed forces—and the world—were very different from what they had been during the 1940s. Benjamin O. Davis Jr. was one of the people who helped make that change.

LIFE EVENTS

1912
Benjamin Oliver Davis Jr. is born in Washington, D.C.

1932
Davis enters West Point.

1943
Davis is placed in command of the Tuskegee Airmen, a black Army Air Force squadron, during World War II.

1948
U.S. President Harry S. Truman orders the armed forces integrated.

1965
Davis becomes the first African American in any U.S. military branch to reach the rank of lieutenant general.

2002
Benjamin O. Davis Jr. dies.

David Farragut
Fearless Commander
(born 1801 • died 1870)

David Farragut's bravery and intelligence during the Civil War made him a national hero. His cry of "Damn the torpedoes! Full speed ahead!" is still remembered today.

A Life at Sea

David Glasgow Farragut was born on July 5, 1801, near Knoxville, Tennessee. His father was a sea captain. When David was very young, his father accepted a job as a sailing master in the Navy. The family moved to New Orleans, Louisiana.

Both of David's parents died when he was young. He was adopted and raised by a family friend named David Porter. Porter was a master commandant in the Navy. Through his influence and encouragement, David was soon at sea himself.

> "I mean to be whipped or to whip my enemy, and not be scared to death."
> —David Farragut

David Farragut left Confederate Virginia to command a Union ship during the Civil War.

David Farragut

During the early 1800s, young boys often served aboard ships. David was only nine years old when he joined the U.S. Navy as a midshipman—someone who is studying to be a naval officer. David fought in the War of 1812.

After the War of 1812, David Farragut served in the Mediterranean Sea and the West Indies. He also took part in a blockade of Mexican ports on the Gulf of Mexico and established the Mare Island Navy Yard in San Francisco. By 1855, he had been promoted to the rank of captain in the Navy.

The Civil War

Farragut had been born in the South. He was living in the southern state of Virginia in 1861, when the Civil War broke out between the northern (Union) and southern (Confederate) states. However, he immediately left his home and declared that he would fight for the Union Army of the north. The Navy was impressed with Farragut's loyalty. He was put in command of a ship called the *Hartford* and told to capture the city of New Orleans.

New Orleans was well-prepared for Farragut's attack. A large barrier had been placed in the harbor to block the passage of northern ships. The shores were lined with forts. In addition, the Confederacy had several warships waiting outside the harbor.

◆ Courage ◆

None of these preparations stopped Farragut. During the night, two Union boats slipped up to the log barrier and cut it free. On April 24, 1862, Farragut's fleet of ships arrived at New Orleans and captured the city. His victory opened the Mississippi River to the Union forces. Farragut became a national hero. In recognition of his accomplishment, he was promoted to rear admiral.

"Damn the Torpedoes!"

For the next two years, Farragut patrolled the Mississippi River. Then, in 1864, he was told to capture Mobile Bay, in Alabama. To reach the bay, Farragut and his ships had to pass through a three-mile-wide channel that was protected by three forts. Once inside the bay, Farragut would have to face several Confederate gunboats.

TOPICAL TIDBIT

Turning the Tide

The importance of naval power in the Civil War is sometimes overlooked. One of the decisive factors in the North's victory was the successful blockade of about 3,500 miles of Confederate coastline by Union ships. The blockade prevented escape and kept the South from importing supplies, which helped turn the tide for the North in the end.

◈ David Farragut ◈

LIFE EVENTS

1801
David Glasgow Farragut is born near Knoxville, Tennessee.

1824
Farragut, an officer in the Navy, is given his first command.

1861
The Civil War breaks out. Farragut leads a successful attack on New Orleans.

1864
Farragut leads his forces in the successful attack on Mobile Bay.

1866
Farragut becomes the first full admiral of the U.S. Navy.

1870
David Farragut dies.

On August 5, he sailed into the channel outside Mobile Bay. There was so much smoke from the guns that it was impossible to see what was going on. So Farragut climbed to the top of the rigging and tied himself to the mast with a rope. Northern newspapers later described how Farragut had gone into battle "lashed to the mast."

At first, things did not go well for Farragut's forces. One of his ships struck a mine and sank. Another ship was stopped by a row of torpedoes in the water. Farragut realized that his fleet was right beneath the firing guns of one of the Confederate forts. There were only two choices: flee or go ahead. Farragut bravely chose to go ahead, sailing the *Hartford* past the stopped ships. When another ship's captain called out a

◈ Courage ◈

warning about the torpedoes, Farragut shouted back, "Damn the torpedoes! Full speed ahead!" His fleet sailed into Mobile Bay. After a fierce three-hour battle, Farragut was able to sink the Confederate ships and gain control of the harbor.

After the Battle of Mobile Bay, Farragut became an even bigger hero than he had been before. In 1864, Congress created the rank of vice admiral for him. In 1866, he was promoted to the newly created rank of admiral. Farragut died on August 14, 1870, while visiting the Portsmouth Navy Yard in New Hampshire. After his death, he was hailed as the Navy's greatest hero. ◈

Geronimo
Apache Warrior
(born 1829 • died 1909)

During his life, Geronimo struggled against enormous odds to win freedom for his Apache tribe. At first, the U.S. authorities thought of him as a savage. In time, however, they came to respect him as a brave warrior who would do anything to defend his people.

Quiet Beginnings

Geronimo's Native American name was Goyathlay, which means "One Who Yawns." He was born into the Chiricahua Apache *(chir-uh-KAH-wuh uh-PATCH-ee)* tribe in 1829, in what is now Clifton, Arizona. His father taught him how to hunt, make tools and weapons, care for horses, and survive in the wilderness. Goyathlay also worked in the fields, helping to grow the tribe's crops of corn, melons, and beans.

When Goyathlay turned 17, he was considered a man and a warrior of the tribe. Soon afterward, he married another member of the tribe. The couple had three children.

A portrait of the great Apache warrior Geronimo after his surrender to the United States Army.

Murder—and Revenge

Goyathlay's quiet life took a sudden change in 1858, when he was about 21 years old. Goyathlay, along with his wife, children, and mother, joined a band of Apaches traveling to Mexico to trade. Many Mexicans hated the Apache. One day, a band of Mexican soldiers led by General Juan Carrasco attacked the camp while the men were away. Goyathlay returned that evening to find that his entire family had been killed by the Mexican soldiers.

Goyathlay returned home and vowed revenge against the Mexicans. For the next few years, he and other Apache warriors took part in raids against Mexican settlers. Goyathlay was such a fierce fighter that he became a hero to the Apache and feared by the Mexicans. The Mexicans called him *Geronimo*, which means "Jerome" in Spanish. The name stuck.

Then the Apache began to have trouble with the Americans. From 1846 to 1848, the U.S. and Mexico fought a war over the territory that is now the southwestern U.S. When the U.S. finally won that war, it promised to stop the Apache from raiding Mexican

> **"I was born on the prairies where the wind blew free and there was nothing to break the light of the sun. I was born where there were no enclosures."**
>
> —Geronimo

◇ Courage ◇

territory. But white miners and settlers began to move onto Apache land in U.S. territory. The U.S. government said that it was time for the Apache to go.

Geronimo and his warriors fought many battles to keep their land. In the end, though, they were no match for the powerful U.S. Army. In 1874, the U.S. government moved the Chiricahua Apache to the San Carlos Reservation in Arizona. Living conditions there were terrible, and the tribe was not allowed to practice its traditional rites. Finally, Geronimo and several other Apache warriors declared war on whites.

A Losing Battle

For the next few years, Geronimo and his fellow Apaches conducted many raids on American settlements. Newspapers around the country wrote stories about his daring deeds, and fierce style of fighting. Soon, the word *Geronimo* entered the English

TOPICAL TIDBIT

The Apache Wars

The wars between the U.S. Army and the Chiricahua Apache were among the fiercest on the frontier. Warriors such as Cochise, Mangas Coloradas, and Geronimo were known for their courage, superior horsemanship, and crafty use of the terrain. They contributed to the Apache reputation for fierceness.

Geronimo

language as a war cry. It became an exclamation that meant "charge!" or "attack!"

But the fighting could not go on forever. The Apache warriors were outnumbered and outgunned. Geronimo returned to the reservation several times, but escaped again each time. Finally, in 1886, he surrendered for good.

Geronimo spent the rest of his life as a prisoner. He and his tribe were sent to reservations in Florida, Alabama, and Oklahoma.

Even when Geronimo was an old man and had been a prisoner for many years, his deeds still fascinated the American people. In 1904, he took part in the World's Fair in St. Louis, Missouri. Crowds of people gathered to meet the old warrior. They stood in line to buy his autograph and photo.

LIFE EVENTS

1829
Geronimo is born Goyathlay, or "One Who Yawns," to the Chiricahua Apache tribe, in what is now Arizona.

1858
Geronimo's mother, wife, and children are killed by Mexican soldiers. Geronimo takes part in raids against Mexico to seek revenge.

1874
The U.S. Army forces thousands of Apaches onto a reservation. Geronimo leads a war against the Army.

1886
Geronimo finally surrenders. He dies in 1909.

◇ Courage ◇

In 1905, President Theodore Roosevelt invited Geronimo to Washington, D.C., to ride in a parade celebrating his election. Thousands of people lined the parade route and cheered for the famous Apache.

The next day, Geronimo met with Roosevelt and asked him to let his people return to their home in Arizona. Roosevelt said no. He was worried that allowing the Native Americans to return would lead to more fighting.

On February 17, 1909, four years after meeting President Roosevelt, Geronimo died. He is still remembered as a fearless warrior who bravely fought for his people's freedom. ◇

Nathan Hale
Only One Life to Give
(born 1755 • died 1776)

Nathan Hale died when he was only 21 years old. But his death made him one of America's most famous and courageous heroes.

An Ordinary Schoolteacher

Nathan Hale was born on June 6, 1755, in Coventry, Connecticut. His parents were Puritans, who stressed the values of religion, hard work, and education. Nathan was a sickly child, but he grew into a strong, athletic young man.

Nathan was schooled by the local minister and soon developed a love of learning. In 1769, 14-year-old Nathan and his older brother entered Yale College. At first, Nathan planned to become a minister. However, after graduating in 1773 at age 18, Nathan Hale decided to become a schoolteacher instead.

Hale taught for one year in East Haddam, Connecticut. After that, he got a job at the Union School in New London, which was a busy seaport on the Connecticut coast. He was a popular teacher with the students and their parents.

◇ Courage ◇

America at War

By 1774, it was clear that the American colonies would soon go to war against Great Britain. Hale joined the Connecticut militia, a volunteer army. When war broke out in April 1775, he was not sure that he wanted to leave his teaching job to fight. Then, in July, he got a letter from a friend, Benjamin Tallmadge, begging him to join the battle. "Was I in your condition," wrote Tallmadge, "I think the more extensive service would be my choice. Our holy religion, the honor of our God, a glorious country, and a happy constitution is what we have to defend." The letter made up Hale's mind.

The next day, Hale accepted a commission as a first lieutenant in a Connecticut regiment. Hale enjoyed military life and did his best to be a good leader.

> **"Let us march immediately, and never lay down our arms until we obtain our independence."**
> —Nathan Hale, after receiving news of the start of the American Revolution

In January 1776, he was promoted to captain and sent to New York City. He spent almost six months there, preparing forts for battle with the British. He also planned an attack on a British ship, an action that won him a personal thank you

"I only regret," replied Nathan Hale, *"that I have but one life to lose for my country."*

from General George Washington, who was commander of the American army.

The British had taken control of Long Island, New York, and planned to invade New York City. General

◈ Courage ◈

Washington needed to find out when the British army planned to attack. Hale volunteered to go behind enemy lines on Long Island to gather information. One of his friends tried to talk him out of the dangerous job. But Hale replied that it was "necessary for the public good." To a young soldier who had not yet seen any fighting, it was also a good chance for adventure.

Captured!

Hale crossed the British lines on Long Island during the second week of September 1776. He pretended to be a schoolteacher looking for work. He managed to obtain important military information.

On the night of September 21, Hale slipped away to Long Island Sound to wait for a boat that was scheduled to pick him up. Lights twinkled from a ship on

TOPICAL TIDBIT

Colonial Spies

General George Washington knew the value of using spies against an enemy. During the French and Indian War (1754-1763), he had served as an officer in the British army. He noted how the French used small bands of Native Americans to spy on his troops. This gave the French a good idea of how many men he had and from which direction they were coming. Later, when he was commanding American forces during the Revolution, Washington used information from spies to help his men defeat the much larger British army.

LIFE EVENTS

1755
Nathan Hale is born in Coventry, Connecticut.

1773
Hale graduates from Yale and becomes a schoolteacher.

1775
Colonists clash with British soldiers at the battle of Lexington and Concord. Hale volunteers with the Seventh Connecticut militia.

1776
While stationed in New York, Hale volunteers for a spy mission. He is caught behind enemy lines and executed by the British.

the sound and Hale signaled his position. Then he realized that the ship was British, not American. Hale tried to escape, but was quickly captured by British soldiers.

That very night, Hale was taken before General William Howe, the British commander. Hale admitted that he was a spy, and was held prisoner in a greenhouse. The next morning, he was hanged as a spy. His last words were reported to be, "I only regret that I have but one life to lose for my country." This speech, and the courage with which he faced death, impressed British soldiers and American citizens alike. Today, Nathan Hale is still remembered as a dedicated, brave man who was willing to pay the highest price of all for his beliefs.

Fannie Lou Hamer
Fighting for Freedom
(born 1917 • died 1977)

Many people fought to win equal rights for black Americans during the civil-rights movement. One of the most courageous of these freedom fighters was a poor, barely educated woman named Fannie Lou Hamer. She risked her life and livelihood to help ensure the right of every African American to vote.

> "The only thing they could do was kill me."
> —Fannie Lou Hamer, on volunteering to register to vote

A Sharecropper's Daughter

Fannie Lou Townsend was born in Montgomery County, Mississippi, on October 6, 1917. She was the youngest of 20 children. Fannie Lou's parents were sharecroppers on a plantation. Sharecropping was a hard life. The family had to pay the plantation's owner for the house they lived in, the crops they grew, and the food they ate. Fannie Lou's earliest memories were of being hungry and tired. The house that the family lived in was a run-down

Fannie Lou Hamer speaks to the U.S. Senate committee about the terrible treatment she received in Mississippi.

wooden shack with a tin roof. At night, Fannie Lou slept on a sack stuffed with dry grass.

While still a small child, Fannie Lou began working in the cotton fields with her parents and siblings. By the time she was six, she was picking 30 pounds of

◆ Courage ◆

cotton a day. There was little time to go to school or play with other children.

Working Toward Equality

In the early 1940s, Fannie Lou Townsend married Perry "Pap" Hamer. She and her husband worked on a plantation until 1962. Then, on one otherwise ordinary day, Fannie Lou Hamer did an extraordinary and brave thing: She tried to register to vote.

Today, we take voting for granted. Until the 1960s, however, black Americans living in the South had to pass special tests and pay a "poll tax" if they wanted to vote. These tests and taxes were designed to keep blacks from voting. They were so unfair that many blacks did not even bother to try registering. Many of those who did register still could not vote,

TOPICAL TIDBIT

Making Change, One Person at a Time

After the Civil War, Southern states began using many methods to keep blacks from voting, including literacy tests, poll taxes, and bullying. Beginning in 1961, the Student Nonviolent Coordinating Committee (SNCC) started a major campaign to register blacks in the South. In a church in the tiny town of Ruleville, Mississippi, a small crowd heard a young preacher named James Bevel ask for volunteers to register. Fannie Lou Hamer raised her hand—and changed her life forever.

because if they tried to do so they were threatened—sometimes even killed—by whites.

Hamer was fired from her job. She and her husband were forced to leave the plantation. Angry white men followed the Hamers everywhere, waving guns and cursing them. Still, Fannie Lou Hamer refused to take her name off the registration list. Instead of giving in to the threats, she fought back: She began organizing voter-registration campaigns all over Mississippi.

Paying the Price

In June 1963, Hamer and several other civil-rights workers took a bus to a voter-registration meeting. On the way home, the bus stopped in the small town of Winona, Mississippi. There, Hamer and the others were arrested, taken to jail, and severely beaten. The beating left Hamer blind in one eye and damaged her feet and her kidneys.

The group was held in jail for three days. Hamer and the other workers were finally allowed to leave after civil-rights leader Martin Luther King Jr. sent his staff to the jail to demand that they be released. Later, Hamer went to Washington, D.C., to tell the government, the newspapers, and the American public about the terrible treatment that black people faced in Mississippi.

"Is This America?"

In 1964, Hamer helped form the Mississippi Freedom Democratic Party (MFDP). A group of MFDP members (64 black, 4 white) traveled to the Democratic National Convention in Atlantic City, New Jersey. Hamer and other MFDP members demanded that they be seated as the official Mississippi delegation that would nominate the presidential candidate. At that time, the Mississippi delegation was all-white; blacks had been purposely excluded.

The MFDP was not allowed to participate fully, but Hamer gave a speech to a Democratic Party committee. It was televised. She told about the beating that she had received in Winona, as well as the threats and hardships that blacks faced every day, just for trying to vote. "Is this America?" she asked. "The land of the free and the home of the brave? Where we have to sleep with our telephones off the hook, because our lives be threatened daily?"

The MFDP did not win seats at the 1964 convention. But its members did participate in the 1968 convention in Chicago. When Hamer took her seat at the 1968 convention, she received a standing ovation.

The Freedom Farm Cooperative

Hamer also worked to help the poor people of Mississippi. In 1969, she organized the Freedom Farm Cooperative, which provided land for poor families to

LIFE EVENTS

1917
Fannie Lou Townsend is born in Montgomery County, Mississippi.

1962
Hamer challenges discrimination by registering to vote.

1963
Hamer and a busload of civil-rights workers are jailed and severely beaten in Mississippi.

1964
Hamer leads the Mississippi Freedom Democratic Party (MFDP) during the Democratic National Convention.

1967
Hamer publishes *To Praise Our Bridges: An Autobiography*.

1968
Hamer formally participates at the Democratic National Convention. She dies in 1977.

grow their own food. She traveled all over the country, giving speeches to raise money and awareness of black poverty and hunger.

Hamer died of cancer on March 15, 1977. She was buried in her native Mississippi. Her tombstone is engraved with one of her favorite sayings: "I'm sick and tired of being sick and tired."

Fannie Lou Hamer rose from humble beginnings. Through her courage and her refusal to give in, she changed the lives of thousands of people.

Wild Bill Hickok
Lawman of the Wild West
(born 1837 • died 1876)

During the 1800s, the western United States was a dangerous place filled with thieves and murderers. One man who was brave enough to battle such risks was Wild Bill Hickok, one of the most famous figures of the American West.

An Early Taste of Adventure

James Butler Hickok was born in Homer, Illinois, on May 27, 1837. The Hickoks' home was a stop on the Underground Railroad. This was a network of people and safe houses that helped runaway slaves make their way to freedom in Northern states or Canada. The Hickoks hid many slaves in their basement. At night, young James often led runaways to their next hiding place.

Hunting was an important part of life in those days. That was no problem for young James, who was an excellent shot. He often put meat on the family's table by shooting deer, rabbits, and other wild animals.

In 1855, when he was 18 years old, James Hickok got a job driving mules along a canal path. One of the older drivers, a man named Charles Hudson, started teasing him, then pushed him into the canal. That made Hickok so angry that he began wrestling with Hudson. The two men fell into the canal. Hickok escaped from the water, but he thought that Hudson had drowned. This upset him so much that he ran away.

Heading West

Hickok walked all the way to Kansas, where he joined the U.S. Army. His shooting was so good that he became the commander's bodyguard. Because he had run away from home, Hickok decided to hide his identity. He told everyone that his name was Bill.

Wild Bill Hickok: frontiersman, marksman, and American legend

Courage

After a few years in the army, Hickok became a stagecoach driver, riding a route from Kansas into the western territories. This was a dangerous job. Stagecoaches were often attacked by thieves or Native Americans. There was also danger from wild animals and buffalo stampedes. Hickok enjoyed his job, however. He always made sure that his wagon arrived safely.

On one rough trip through the Rocky Mountains, Hickok was attacked by a grizzly bear. He managed to kill the bear, but he was seriously injured. It looked like Hickok would die, but the tough young man survived.

> **"Leave town on the eastbound train, the westbound train, or go North [to Boot Hill, the cemetery] in the morning."**
> —Marshal Bill Hickok, warning troublemakers that he would hunt them down

The Army, and More Adventures

In 1861, the Civil War began. Hickok joined the North's Union Army. He was assigned to lead Army wagon trains. On one trip to Missouri, he saw an angry mob about to hang a young man. To stop them, Hickok drew his gun and pointed it at the mob's leaders. The mob quickly disappeared without

◆ **Wild Bill Hickok** ◆

a shot being fired. Hickok's bravery became the talk of the town. Someone yelled, "Good for you, Wild Bill!"—and Hickok had a new nickname.

Later, Hickok became a spy for the Union Army. He loved the dangerous job of slipping behind enemy lines to find out what the other side was doing. On one trip, Hickok was captured and ordered to be executed as a spy. The night before his execution, he broke free, attacked his guard, and got away in the guard's clothes. Word of Hickok's daring escape made him a hero in the Northern states.

Laying Down the Law

After the Civil War ended in 1865, Hickok was asked to be the law officer at Fort Riley, Kansas. His job was to restore order and prevent soldiers from stealing horses and running away. This dangerous job paid $75 a month. With Hickok in charge, Fort Riley became a much safer, calmer place.

In 1869, some people from Hays City, Kansas asked Hickok to be their marshal. He was often shot at and threatened, but he won every gun battle and cleaned up the town.

Hickok later worked as the marshal in Abilene, Kansas, which was another rough frontier town. One night, he killed one of his best friends by mistake during a shootout. Because of that tragedy, he quit his job.

◆ Courage ◆

A Showman to the End

During the 1870s, Wild Bill Hickok was featured in many magazine articles and novels. He also joined Buffalo Bill's Wild West show for a couple of years. Those exciting shows starred well-known Western heroes. They toured the country staging fake battles as well as rodeos and buffalo roundups.

In 1876, Hickok went to Deadwood, a town in the Dakota Territory, to look for gold. By this time, he was tired of fighting, and his eyesight was failing. "My shooting days are over," he wrote to a friend.

Still, the outlaws there were afraid that he would be appointed marshal and clean up the town. Determined to stay, they looked for someone to kill the famous lawman. Several gunman were too afraid to try. Finally, a man named Jack McCall

TOPICAL TIDBIT

Dead Man's Hand

On August 2, 1876, Wild Bill Hickok joined a poker game in Carl Mann's Saloon in Deadwood. Carelessly, he took a seat with his back to the door—which he had always been careful not to do. When Jack McCall shot him, he fell backward and his "hand"—the group of cards he was holding—hit the floor. Hickok's fellow players looked at the cards: He had been holding a pair of aces and a pair of eights. From then on, throughout the West, a hand of aces and eights was known as the Dead Man's Hand.

Wild Bill Hickok

LIFE EVENTS

1837
James Butler Hickok is born in Homer, Illinois.

1855
A fistfight causes Hickok to flee west to Kansas.

1861
The Civil War begins and Hickok joins the Union Army. Facing down an angry mob earns him the nickname Wild Bill.

1865
Hickok outdraws gunman Dave Tutt in Springfield, Missouri. A story in *Harper's New Monthly Magazine* begins to spread his legend.

1869
Hickok is elected marshal of Hays City, Kansas.

1876
Hickok is shot and killed in Deadwood, Dakota Territory.

agreed to do it. On August 2, 1876, Jack McCall shot Wild Bill Hickok in the back of the head while Hickok was playing cards. Hickok was 39 years old.

Wild Bill Hickok's reputation has long outlived him. Today, he is still remembered as a courageous hero of the American West who was not afraid to fight for justice.

Anne Hutchinson
Champion of Religious Freedom
(born 1591 • died 1643)

One of the founding principles of the United States was that everyone would be able to practice whatever religion that he or she wanted to. However, during colonial days, this was not always allowed. Anne Hutchinson was someone who suffered because of her beliefs. Her courage helped bring the idea of religious freedom to all Americans.

A Quiet Life

Anne Hutchinson did not seem like the type of person who would cause trouble. She was born Anne Marbury in England in 1591. In 1612, she married a merchant named William Hutchinson. In 1634, the Hutchinsons moved their family to Boston, which—at that time—was a small town in the Massachusetts Bay Colony. Most of the people who lived there were members of a strict religious movement called Puritanism. Puritans had many strict rules to follow. They strongly believed that the

In 1637, Anne Hutchinson was put on trial for her beliefs.

only true Christians were people who followed all of these rules to the letter.

William Hutchinson had been a rich landowner in England. When he, Anne, and their children moved to the American colonies, they soon became one of the most well-known and most popular families in Boston. Anne Hutchinson worked as a midwife, delivering babies, and she had many friends among the women of the town.

Trouble!

Anne Hutchinson was a very religious person. Her father had been a minister, and she had read the Bible and other religious works. She decided to share her views on religious questions with Boston's women. She began holding meetings in her home. During those meetings, the women discussed what their minister had said in church on Sunday, and what they thought about it. They also talked about how they believed a person should worship God.

> "As I do understand it, laws, commands, rules . . . are for those who have not the light which makes plain the pathway. He who has God's grace in his heart cannot go astray."
> —Anne Hutchinson

Anne Hutchinson

During the meetings, Hutchinson told her friends that she believed in a "covenant of grace" from God for each person. (A *covenant* is a formal, solemn, unbreakable promise.) She said that people had to talk to God themselves. They could not rely on what the minister said. Hutchinson also said that going to church was not important. She encouraged people to think for themselves and find their own ways to worship God.

The leaders of the Massachusetts Bay Colony got very angry when they heard what Hutchinson was saying. They thought that she was encouraging people to make up their own rules and do whatever they felt was right. Church leaders worried that people would stop listening to them and stop attending services. Soon Hutchinson was in a lot of trouble.

At first, her friends stood by her. One of her strongest supporters was a well-known and respected minister named John Cotton. Later, however, Massachusetts got a new governor, John Winthrop. He hated Hutchinson's ideas. Under pressure from Winthrop, members of the community began to turn against Hutchinson. Finally, even John Cotton said that she was wrong.

But Anne Hutchinson refused to change her beliefs. In 1637, she was put on trial by Governor Winthrop. When Hutchinson said that Winthrop's rules were "against the word of God," she was convicted by the

◆ Courage ◆

General Court. Hutchinson was banished from (forced to leave) Massachusetts forever. However, since it was the middle of winter and Hutchinson was expecting a baby, she did not leave right away. She was allowed to stay in Boston until the spring.

Freedom—Then a Violent End

Early in 1638, Hutchinson and her family left Boston and moved to the neighboring colony of Rhode Island. Rhode Island had been founded by Roger Williams, who also had been banished from Massachusetts for his religious beliefs. In Rhode Island, Hutchinson was finally able to worship as she pleased.

Some of her friends and supporters joined the Hutchinsons in Rhode Island. Together, they founded

TOPICAL TIDBIT

Mary Barrett Dyer

One of the people who followed Anne Hutchinson to Rhode Island was Mary Barrett Dyer. Like Hutchinson, Dyer strongly believed in religious freedom. Eventually, Dyer became a member of the Society of Friends, also called the Quakers, and returned to Massachusetts to be a Quaker missionary. When Massachusetts passed anti-Quaker laws, Dyer's life was in danger. She was banished twice and almost hanged for her beliefs, but she kept going back. In 1660, she was hanged, but her death made more people see the importance of religious freedom.

Anne Hutchinson

LIFE EVENTS

1591
Anne Marbury is born in England.

1634
Now Anne Hutchinson, she moves with her family to the Massachusetts Bay Colony.

1636
Hutchinson comes into conflict with John Winthrop, the governor of Massachusetts.

1637
Winthrop puts Hutchinson on trial for opposing the Puritan ministers. Convicted and banished, Hutchinson moves to the colony of Rhode Island in 1638.

1643
Hutchinson and her family, living on Long Island, are killed by Mahican Indians.

the town of Portsmouth. The Hutchinsons lived there for the next four years, until William Hutchinson died in 1642. After that, Anne Hutchinson moved her family to Pelham Bay on Long Island, New York. They lived quietly there, in a small cabin in the wilderness. A few months later, in 1643, Hutchinson and her family were attacked by Indians who burned their home. Most of her family was killed.

Anne Hutchinson may have been banished from Massachusetts, but she was not forgotten there. Today, a statue of her stands on Beacon Hill in Boston. It reminds everyone of this woman, who bravely stood up for her beliefs.

Andrew Jackson
President of the Common People
(born 1767 • died 1845)

Until Andrew Jackson, all U.S. presidents had come from wealthy, well-educated families. But Jackson was a rough, tough soldier with humble origins. His courage, energy, and intelligence made him one of the most popular and important presidents in history.

Backwoods Beginnings

Andrew Jackson was born on March 15, 1767, in South Carolina. His family had moved to America from Ireland two years earlier, and lived in a log cabin in the wilderness. Andrew's father died soon after Andrew was born. His mother moved in with her sister, and Andrew grew up in a large household full of cousins.

From the start, Andrew was tough. If anyone pushed him around, he was quick to fight back. He soon had a reputation as a strong, hot-tempered, brave fighter.

Andrew learned many things during his childhood. He learned to hunt, fish, and trap wild

As president of the United States, Andrew Jackson was well liked by the people.

animals—skills important for people living in the wilderness. He was also very intelligent, despite having received very little schooling.

Andrew was nine years old when the American Revolution began in 1776. When he was 13, he joined the army and took part in several battles. He also was captured by the British and put to work for them. When he refused to clean the boots of a British officer, the man slashed him across the hand and

◇ Courage ◇

head with his sword. Andrew Jackson proudly carried the scars from those wounds for the rest of his life.

The Battle of New Orleans

After the war ended, Jackson became a teacher, then a lawyer. In 1788, he and some friends traveled to Nashville, Tennessee, to practice law. They believed that the large number of settlers moving into Tennessee would need legal help.

Soon Jackson was a rich, successful frontier lawyer. His abilities helped him win the election as Tennessee's representative to the U.S. Congress in 1796. Later, he became a judge on Tennessee's superior court. He held this post for six years. He quickly earned a reputation as an honest, fair, and dignified justice.

> **"One man with courage makes a majority."**
> —a favorite saying of Andrew Jackson

When the War of 1812 began, 45-year-old Jackson took command of 2,500 Tennessee volunteers. His men called him "Old Hickory" in honor of his courage, because hickory is the toughest wood in the wilderness. He won important battles against Native American tribes fighting on the British side. However, his greatest battle was against the British in New Orleans.

Jackson and his soldiers arrived in New Orleans on December 2, 1814. Three weeks later, 6,000

Andrew Jackson

British troops invaded the city. For two weeks, Jackson's outnumbered men fought the British in small battles. Then, on January 8, 1815, the final battle took place. It ended with a tremendous American victory. Fewer than 35 Americans were killed and around 50 were injured, compared to around 300 British dead and nearly 2,000 injured.

On to the White House

After the war, Jackson became a U.S. senator from Tennessee. In 1828, the popular and honored hero was elected the seventh president of the United States. He was the first president to come from a poor family, and he was hugely popular with the common people. Jackson said that the White House belonged to the people. He welcomed people to visit the White

---

TOPICAL TIDBIT

"A Corrupt Bargain"

Andrew Jackson first ran for president in 1824. The election was so close that the House of Representatives had to decide the winner. Jackson had the most votes of four candidates. However, some experts believe that the candidate with the second-most votes, John Quincy Adams, made a deal with the third-place candidate, Henry Clay. They think Clay gave his votes to Adams, so Adams became president. Jackson and his supporters were so angry, they accused the new president of making a "corrupt [rotten] bargain." Four years later, they beat John Quincy Adams and had their revenge.

◆ Courage ◆

House and come shake his hand any time.

Jackson strongly believed that each state had the right to determine its own laws. However, he also thought that each state had to be loyal to the U.S. When South Carolina threatened to ignore a federal law, Jackson said that he would send the army to enforce it. "Our federal Union—it must be preserved," he said. South Carolina backed down, and the Union was saved.

Jackson won a second term as president in 1832. After he left office in 1837, he retired to his plantation in Tennessee. He died eight years later, on June 8, 1845. Andrew Jackson was hailed as a courageous champion of the people, and is still admired today. ◆

LIFE EVENTS

1767
Andrew Jackson is born in the Waxhaws region of South Carolina.

1780
At 13, Jackson joins the American army during the American Revolution.

1788
Jackson moves to Nashville, Tennessee.

1796
Jackson is elected U.S. Representative from Tennessee.

1815
During the War of 1812, Jackson leads U.S. troops to victory at the Battle of New Orleans.

1828
Jackson wins the first of two terms as president of the U.S. He dies in 1845.

Joan of Arc
Military Hero, Martyr, Saint
(born about 1412 • died 1431)

Joan of Arc was a young Catholic woman in 15th-century France who changed the course of history. She claimed to receive messages from God that told her to lead French soldiers against the invading English army. Joan led her troops to important victories for France. She inspired her fellow citizens to rise up against the English. Later, she was executed for her beliefs. Today, she is recognized as a Catholic saint.

Growing Up in 15th-century France

Joan was born around 1412 in Domrémy, France. The daughter of peasant farmers, she could neither read nor write. At that time, England and France were Catholic nations. Although each nation had its own king, both looked to the Pope (leader of the Catholic church) to learn God's will. People who disagreed with Catholic practices or had different ideas were called *heretics (HER-uh-tiks)*. Heretics were punished, tortured, and executed.

Joan was only 17 years old when she led French troops into battle against England.

When Joan was growing up, France was at war with England. France's King Charles VI died in 1422, and his eldest son, the Dauphin *(DAW-fun)*, wanted to become king. However, England's king, Henry VI, wanted to take the French throne. Some French citizens supported France, others supported England. The war raged on.

Joan of Arc

> "Je suis envoyée de par Dieu, le Roi du Ciel." ["I am sent here by God, the King of Heaven."]
>
> —Joan of Arc, in her first letter to the English, March 22, 1429

Heavenly Voices

Joan was a very religious girl. When she was 13 years old, she began hearing voices. Sometimes she saw a great beam of light when the voices spoke to her. Joan believed that the voices were those of Catholic saints giving her messages from God. When Joan was 16, the voices told her that God wanted her to help the Dauphin become the new king of France.

Joan wanted to see the Dauphin, but was stopped by his guards. They could not imagine why a young girl thought that she could help the future king. Many people doubted that Joan was being sent by God. Some thought that she was a witch. In 1429, Joan was finally allowed to see the Dauphin. She convinced him that she was, indeed, sent by God. He believed her and sent her into battle as the leader of her own soldiers.

Leading her troops into battle in Orléans, France, Joan wore a suit of armor, used a sword, and fought alongside her men. In a surprising victory, the French drove the English out of the area. Joan became known as the Maid of Orléans. She continued to fight, and win, in other areas of France. Her courage, spirit, and impressive victories helped strengthen the French cause. No longer did the French feel defeated. They were eager to take back their nation. Joan helped the Dauphin become King Charles VII on July 17, 1429.

Heretic or Saint?

Before she knew it, Joan had become a national hero. The English did not like this at all. They were outraged that she was a woman who wore men's clothes and claimed to be sent by God. The English accused her of practicing witchcraft.

In May 1430, Joan was captured and sold to the English. She was later tried for heresy. Her crime was that she claimed to receive direct communication from God. Catholics believed that God communicated directly only through the Pope. Joan did not have a lawyer to defend her. She was repeatedly questioned and threatened with torture. She was found guilty and

---

TOPICAL TIDBIT

Condemned for Her Clothes

During Joan's trial, much was made of her wearing men's clothing. In fact, officials even added that to her list of crimes. They said that for a woman to insist on wearing men's clothing was an "act against God."

◈ Joan of Arc ◈

burned at the stake on May 30, 1431, in Rouen, France. She was only 19 years old. Charles VII did not come to her aid.

Saint Joan

About 20 years after Joan's death, Charles VII looked into her case. Several years later, under direction from the Pope, the case was reviewed. Joan was found innocent of all charges. Recognizing that Joan of Arc had courageously died for her beliefs, the Catholic church proclaimed her a saint in 1920, nearly 500 years after her death. Today, Joan of Arc is known as one of the most famous heroes in history. ◈

LIFE EVENTS

About 1412
Joan is born in Domrémy, France.

1429
Joan meets with the Dauphin of France, who grants her an army. She wins key battles against the English. Following Joan's efforts, the Dauphin becomes Charles VII, King of France.

1430
Joan is captured and sold to the English.

1431
Joan is convicted of being a witch. She is burned at the stake in England.

Francis Marion
The Swamp Fox
(born 1732 • died 1795)

For most of his life, Francis Marion was an average farmer. Then the American Revolution turned him into a skilled fighter—and an American hero.

An Ordinary Life

Not much is known about Francis Marion's early years. Historians believe that he was born in 1732, in Berkeley County, South Carolina. For most of his life, Marion farmed the rich South Carolina land.

Around 1760, many men in South Carolina formed a militia (volunteer army) to fight the Cherokee Indians. Marion joined the militia, and served until 1761. Then he went back to farming.

South Carolina at War

In 1775, the American colonies were moving toward war against Great Britain. Marion took part in South Carolina's first revolutionary convention. The convention organized two military units of men to fight against the British. Marion was put in charge of one of those units.

Francis Marion, known as "the Swamp Fox," escapes British soldiers during the American Revolution.

In September 1775, Marion and his men chased the British fleet out of Charleston's harbor. Getting rid of the British ships turned out to be a huge help to the colony during the war.

◈ Courage ◈

For the next three years, Marion organized and trained his men. Then, in September 1779, he took part in a campaign to drive the British out of Savannah, Georgia. The colonists were defeated. Marion publicly announced that if his forces had been allowed to strike more quickly, they might have been able to capture the city.

"The Swamp Fox"

Things got even worse for the American side in 1780, when the British captured Charleston. Marion was one of the few officers to escape. He quickly gathered about 200 of the best men he could find. The group called itself Marion's Brigade, and set out to attack the British.

> "Well now, Colonel Doyle, look sharp. For you shall presently feel the edge of our swords!"
> —Francis Marion's warning to the British commander
> (according to biographer Mason Locke Weems)

Because the British army was so much larger, Marion knew that he and his men couldn't face it head-on. The only way to fight it was to strike quickly and withdraw before the British could react. For the next two years, he and his men used the Carolina swamps as their base. Rushing out from their hiding place, Marion's Brigade launched many surprise attacks on the British army. Then they disappeared back into the swamps.

Francis Marion

Conditions in the swamp were harsh. Like his men, Marion slept on the ground, without any blankets or tents to protect him. But the small army's methods worked. Colonel Banastre Tarleton, the most feared British leader in South Carolina, was forever frustrated that Marion kept slipping through his fingers. "As for the . . . old fox," the colonel said, "the devil himself could not catch him!" From then on, Marion was known as "the Swamp Fox."

Later, Marion helped other military leaders capture British posts along the Santee River. He also commanded a unit that helped drive the British out of South Carolina for good.

After the War

When the American Revolution ended in 1783, Marion was thanked by Congress for his "wise, gallant, and decided conduct." Congress also gave

---

TOPICAL TIDBIT

Guerrilla Warfare

Francis Marion's band of "irregulars" practiced a kind of fighting called guerrilla *(guh-RIL-uh)* warfare. Small armies throughout history have used this strategy to strike at, and often defeat, larger armies. The American colonists had to rely on methods such as this to beat the British troops, who were more numerous and had much better weapons.

Courage

him a pension (retirement money) for his military service. Marion went on to serve as a state senator from 1782-1790. During his terms, he was known as a dignified, polite, and kind-hearted man. He spoke out against harsh punishments for South Carolina residents who had helped the British during the war.

Francis Marion died on February 27, 1795. His determination and courage during one of the most dramatic periods in U.S. history has made him a legend.

LIFE EVENTS

1732
Francis Marion is born in South Carolina.

1775
Marion is a delegate to the South Carolina Provincial Congress.

1776
American independence is declared. Marion, a captain in the 2nd South Carolina Regiment, drives the British out of Charleston harbor.

1780
Marion's Brigade attacks the British from hiding places in the Carolina swamps.

1783
The American Revolution ends. Marion later serves as a state senator and commander at Fort Johnson. He dies in 1795.

John McCain
Bravery Under Pressure
(born 1936)

John McCain has shown courage in many forms—as a naval pilot, a prisoner of war, and a politician. No matter what situation life has placed him in, he has always stood firmly for what he believes.

Growing Up in the Navy

John Sidney McCain III was born on August 29, 1936, in the Panama Canal Zone. His father and grandfather were both commanders in the U.S. Navy. It probably was no surprise when John also decided on a naval career.

Young John did not take school very seriously, however. He much preferred having good times with his friends. Even when he was admitted to the U.S. Naval Academy in Annapolis, Maryland, and faced more serious studies, John did not settle down. When John McCain graduated from the Naval Academy in 1958, he was fifth from the bottom of his class.

Senator John McCain takes a reporter's question during a 1998 news conference.

John McCain

Trouble in Vietnam

McCain trained to be a naval aviator (flier). He was a good pilot, and soon earned a reputation for keeping calm under pressure. Once, while McCain was sitting in his fighter jet on the deck of the aircraft carrier *Forrestal*, another jet accidentally fired a missile that hit his plane. He escaped—then rushed back to help injured airmen.

During the 1960s, the U.S. was fighting a war in Vietnam, a country in Asia. John McCain, by now a veteran pilot, volunteered for duty. Vietnam would prove to be the most challenging and difficult experience of his life.

In 1967, McCain's plane was shot down over Hanoi, North Vietnam's capital city. That was enemy territory. (The U.S. was fighting on South Vietnam's side.) McCain was seriously injured when the plane crashed into a lake. Then a crowd of people dragged him out of the water and attacked him. By the time policemen pulled McCain away from the crowd, he had broken bones and other injuries.

> "I had a lot of time [in the prisoner-of-war camp] to think and I came to the conclusion that one of the most important things in life is to make some contribution to your country."
>
> —John McCain

◈ Courage ◈

At first, he was taken to a prison hospital, but his injuries were not treated. He was in such bad shape that many people thought that he would die. Then his captors found out that his father was an American naval hero. After that, his injuries were treated. McCain eventually left the hospital and was sent to the main prison.

The conditions in the prison were harsh. Prisoners were tortured and beaten. The prisoners jokingly called the place Hanoi Hilton. (*Hilton* is the name of a chain of fancy hotels—nothing like what the prisoners actually faced.) In prison, McCain was frequently beaten and tortured. His guards wanted him to say that he was a spy and that the U.S. was an evil country. McCain refused to do so for a long time. But the torture finally became too much for him. To his great

TOPICAL TIDBIT

The U.S.S. *Forrestal*

In 1967, Lieutenant Commander John McCain was assigned to the aircraft carrier U.S.S. *Forrestal*, off the coast of Vietnam. On July 29, as he was preparing to take off on a bombing mission, a missile was accidentally fired from a nearby plane, striking one of his fuel tanks. McCain just barely escaped from his burning plane. Then, as he tried to help a fellow pilot whose flight suit had burst into flames, another explosion knocked him back 10 feet. In all, 134 men died that day. It was the worst noncombat-related accident in U.S. naval history.

shame, he signed a paper that said that he was a spy, even though it was not true.

Because McCain's family was important in the U.S. military, the North Vietnamese offered to release him. However, McCain thought that it was unfair for him to go home ahead of other prisoners who had been at the Hanoi Hilton for a longer time. So he refused the offer of release. McCain and many other prisoners of war were finally released in 1973, when the U.S. agreed to stop the war. McCain had been imprisoned for five and a half years.

Taking Up Politics

McCain received many awards for his bravery in Vietnam, including the Silver Star, Legion of Merit, Purple Heart, and Distinguished Flying Cross. He retired from the U.S. Navy in 1981, after a 22-year career. Then he decided to serve his country in a different way—as an elected official. McCain first represented Arizona as a Republican in the House of Representatives from 1983 to 1986. In 1986, he was elected to the U.S. Senate.

As a senator, McCain has served on the Senate's Armed Services Committee and the Indian Affairs Committee, working to help veterans and Native Americans. He also has worked hard for campaign finance reforms. McCain believes that there are too many special-interest groups (powerful, wealthy people and industries) influencing government. This means that ordinary people are less likely to be heard.

In 1999, McCain decided to run for president. Although many Americans responded to McCain's ideas, he did not win enough votes to successfully challenge George W. Bush for the Republican nomination. After McCain dropped out of the race, however, he continued to spread his message.

Senator McCain has gained increasing support in the U.S. Congress for his campaign finance reform program. His courage—both in the military and in politics—is an inspiration to anyone faced with a challenge.

LIFE EVENTS

1936
John Sidney McCain III is born in the Panama Canal Zone.

1958
McCain graduates from the United States Naval Academy.

1967
McCain is shot down over North Vietnam. He spends the next five and a half years as a prisoner of war.

1982
McCain is elected to the U.S. House of Representatives.

1986
McCain is elected to the U.S. Senate.

1999
McCain runs for president of the United States.

2003
Senator McCain continues to call for campaign finance reform in Congress.

Eddie Rickenbacker
Flying Ace
(born 1890 • died 1973)

Eddie Rickenbacker became famous as one of the most daring fighter pilots of World War I. His bravery and style made him one of the war's most popular figures.

Fast Cars

Edward Vernon Rickenbacker was born in Columbus, Ohio, on October 8, 1890. His parents had emigrated from Switzerland. When Eddie was 13, his father was killed in a construction accident. To help support his family, Eddie left school. He lied about his age to get a job in a glass factory.

Eddie loved machines and wanted to work with them. He worked in a garage, and later for a car manufacturer. By the time he was 17, Eddie was a well-paid auto mechanic and salesman, even though he had only a sixth-grade education.

In those days, car manufacturers often promoted their cars by racing them. Eddie enjoyed racing, and

Courage

was soon a star in the field. When Eddie was 21, he got his first chance to race in the famous Indianapolis 500. By 1916, he was one of the nation's top-ranking racers, and had set a world record for speed driving.

Taking to the Skies

World War I had broken out in Europe in 1914, but the U.S. did not join the fighting until April 1917. One month later, Rickenbacker was getting ready to compete in the Indianapolis 500 once again. But instead, he chose to serve his country. General John J. Pershing was leading the American Expeditionary Forces (AEF) in World War I.

> "I'll fight like a wildcat."
> —Eddie Rickenbacker's motto

Pershing wanted Rickenbacker to be his driver in France. Rickenbacker jumped at this rare chance.

While in France, Rickenbacker also worked for Colonel William "Billy" Mitchell, the chief air officer for the AEF. Mitchell encouraged Rickenbacker to apply for pilot training. In March 1918, Rickenbacker received his first assignment as a combat pilot.

Airplanes had been around only 15 years in 1918. World War I was the first time they were used in combat. Aerial combat—planes doing battle in the

Eddie Rickenbacker sits atop a World War I-era fighter plane.

air—was known as dogfighting. Rickenbacker's first dogfight was in April 1918, when he shot down a German plane. Soon afterward, he was nearly shot down himself by the enemy. He managed to fly his damaged plane back to the American lines before crash-landing on his own airfield.

◇ Courage ◇

In September, Rickenbacker was promoted to captain and put in command of a squadron of fighter planes. At first, the other pilots didn't like him because he was from a poor, working-class background. However, Rickenbacker soon won their respect. The other pilots especially appreciated the fact that their captain never asked them to take any risks that he wouldn't take himself.

By the end of the war, Rickenbacker was a flying ace. He had achieved 26 victories against German airplanes and balloons—more than any other pilot. He was called America's "ace of aces."

Rickenbacker returned home to a hero's welcome. He was awarded the Congressional Medal of Honor, the highest honor in the U.S. military.

TOPICAL TIDBIT

Colonel Billy Mitchell

During World War I and for many years afterward, the U.S. did not have an Air Force that was separate from the Army and Navy. Colonel Billy Mitchell fought the War Department officials for years to create one. He made a lot of people angry along the way. In 1925, Mitchell publicly criticized the War Department for losing a Navy airship, and the Army put him on trial. However, Billy Mitchell remained a hero to many Americans. He was awarded a special Congressional Medal of Honor in 1946. His dream of an independent U.S. Air Force finally came to pass in 1947.

Eddie Rickenbacker

Parades and other events were held in his honor. The "ace of aces" also published a book about his wartime experiences.

After the War

After leaving the armed forces, Rickenbacker continued his work in the fields of automobiles and aviation. He worked for General Motors, and later became general manager of the company's Eastern Air Lines. When General Motors decided to sell the airline in 1938, Rickenbacker was able to raise enough money to buy it. Under his control, Eastern grew from a small airline into one of the nation's most successful carriers.

Crash Landing

During World War II, the U.S. government called Rickenbacker back into service. He took a job inspecting air bases all over the world. One of those journeys turned into a dangerous adventure. In October 1942, Rickenbacker and seven other men were aboard a B-17 bomber from Hawaii to New Guinea. The plane crashed into the Pacific Ocean. He and the other men were stranded on rafts in the middle of the ocean.

Everyone in America thought that Eddie Rickenbacker was dead. However, after drifting for about three weeks and living on rainwater, a sea gull, and some fish, the survivors—including Rickenbacker—

Courage

were spotted by an American plane and rescued. Only one of the men died. In 1943, Rickenbacker published a book about that ordeal, called *Seven Came Through*.

After World War II, Rickenbacker returned to Eastern Air Lines, where he served as director and chairman of the board until 1963. He died in Zurich, Switzerland, on July 23, 1973. He was 82 years old.

Eddie Rickenbacker's work with Eastern Airlines helped shape the future of commercial aviation. But he will always be remembered as a fearless and courageous flying ace and war hero.

LIFE EVENTS

1890
Edward Vernon Rickenbacker is born in Columbus, Ohio.

1918
Rickenbacker fights the first of many dogfights over Europe during World War I.

1919
Fighting the Flying Circus, Rickenbacker's book about World War I, is published.

1930
Rickenbacker is awarded the Congressional Medal of Honor.

1942
Rickenbacker's plane is forced down over the Pacific. He and six others survive 24 days at sea.

1973
Rickenbacker dies in Zurich, Switzerland.

Sally Ride
First American Woman in Space
(born 1951)

Until June 18, 1983, every U.S. astronaut who went into space was a man. Sally Ride changed that by becoming the first American woman to leave Earth and soar into space.

An Active Childhood

Sally Kristen Ride was born on May 26, 1951, in Encino, California. Her parents were teachers. Sally and her younger sister were always encouraged to do their best, even if that meant acting differently from how society expected girls to behave.

Sally loved sports. She often talked her way into playing football or baseball with neighborhood boys. Her favorite sport was tennis. By the time she was in high school, she was nationally ranked. Tennis star Billie Jean King saw Sally play and suggested that she quit school and turn professional. However, Sally had many other interests that she wanted to explore.

One of those interests was science. Sally took as many science classes as she could in high school.

Sally Ride, shown in a NASA portrait, became the first American woman in space.

Later, she attended California's Stanford University, partly because it had an excellent tennis team, and partly because it had one of the best science programs in the country. After graduating in 1973 with a degree in physics, she went on to get her master's degree and PhD at Stanford.

Reaching the Stars

One day in 1978, Sally Ride was reading the UCLA newspaper. She saw an article that said that NASA was looking for scientists who wanted to be astronauts. Ride rushed to apply. So did more than 8,000 other people. Out of that group, NASA chose 35 finalists—only six of whom were women, including Ride. They went to the Johnson Space Center near Houston, Texas, for interviews and medical exams. A month later, Ride was chosen to join the space program.

> "The thing that I'll remember most about the [space] flight is that it was fun. In fact, I'm sure it was the most fun I'll ever have in my life."
> —Sally Ride

Ride went through tough physical and mental training to become an astronaut. In 1979, she qualified as a mission specialist—someone who conducts experiments and does other tasks on space-shuttle flights.

As one of NASA's first female astronauts, Ride faced some unusual problems. For example, in the early days of the program, astronauts were not issued pajamas for space flights. They just wore their underwear. But with Ride aboard, all the astronauts wore "space shorts and T-shirts."

On June 18, 1983, Sally Ride was launched into space aboard the shuttle *Challenger*. As the flight engineer, her job was to make sure that all the

Sally Ride waves to reporters as she and other crew members prepare to board the space shuttle Challenger *in 1983.*

Sally Ride

shuttle's mechanical systems were working properly. She also worked with another astronaut to launch two communications satellites.

Ride loved flying into space. She was amazed at just how beautiful it was. She says that she often had a hard time concentrating on her job, because all she wanted to do was look out the window. The view, she said, was breathtaking.

Ride's mission was a huge success. She became a national celebrity. But she did not consider herself an extraordinary person. When asked about her position as America's first female astronaut, she always pointed out that she was a scientist, not a female scientist.

In October 1984, Ride made a second *Challenger* flight. Once again, she launched a satellite.

TOPICAL TIDBIT

The *Challenger*

On Sally Ride's second *Challenger* flight in 1984, she was not the only female astronaut. On that mission, her childhood friend, Kathryn Sullivan, became the first American woman to walk in space. The last *Challenger* flight made history of another kind. Christa McAuliffe, a schoolteacher, had been chosen to be the first private citizen sent into space. On January 28, 1986, millions of people watched on TV as McAuliffe and her fellow astronauts prepared for takeoff. Moments later came a shocking sight: The *Challenger* blew up, killing McAuliffe and her six fellow passengers.

Back to Earth

After her historic flights, Ride continued to work for NASA. She was appointed to the presidential committee that investigated the *Challenger* disaster, after the shuttle exploded during takeoff in 1986. In 1987, she created NASA's Office of Exploration.

Ride left NASA in 1987 and taught science at Stanford University. Two years later, she became a physics professor at the University of California at San Diego, and director of the California Space Institute. In 2003, Ride was inducted into the Astronaut Hall of Fame at the Kennedy Space Center.

Throughout her life, Sally Ride has been a role model for young people. She has shown them that through courage and hard work, dreams can come true.

LIFE EVENTS

1951
Sally Kristen Ride is born in Los Angeles, California.

1961
NASA puts the first American, Alan Shepard, into space.

1963
Valentina Tereshkova, a Russian cosmonaut, orbits Earth, becoming the first woman in space.

1983
Ride's space-shuttle flight makes her the first American woman in space.

1987
Ride creates the Office of Exploration at NASA.

2003
Sally Ride is inducted into the Astronaut Hall of Fame.

Sacagawea
Guide to the West
(born about 1787 • died 1812 or 1884)

In 1804, Meriwether Lewis and William Clark set out to explore what is now northwestern U.S. Early in their two-year journey, they met Sacagawea *(sak-uh-juh-WEE-uh)*. The young Native American woman became their interpreter and friend—and an essential part of their expedition.

A Young Wife and Mother

Little is known about Sacagawea's childhood. A member of the Shoshone tribe, she probably was born in Idaho around 1787. When she was about 12 years old, she and several other Shoshone women and children were captured by the Hidatsa, another Native American tribe. Sacagawea was then sold as a slave to an Indian tribe that lived along the Missouri River. That tribe, in turn, sold Sacagawea to a Canadian fur trapper named Toussaint Charbonneau *(too-SAHN shar-buh-NOH)*.

Charbonneau had several Native American wives. Sacagawea became one of them. She gave birth to their son, Jean Baptiste (known as Pompey), in

Sacagawea guided Lewis and Clark's expedition through the western territory of the United States.

◇ Sacagawea ◇

1805. Sacagawea, Charbonneau, and Pompey were living at Fort Mandan, a military camp in what is now North Dakota. That is where they met the men who would change the young woman's life.

The Journey West

In 1804, President Thomas Jefferson had sent Meriwether Lewis and William Clark to explore the northwestern U.S. They were to draw maps, befriend Native American tribes, and draw pictures and collect samples of plants and animals they found along the way.

> "We find [that Sacagawea helps us with] the Indians, as to our friendly intentions. A woman with a party of men is a token of peace."
>
> —William Clark, in his journal

When Lewis and Clark reached what is now North Dakota, they realized that they would need horses to cross the Rocky Mountains. They would have to buy the horses from the Shoshone Indians. But the explorers did not speak the Shoshone language. They needed an interpreter to help them. When they heard about Charbonneau and his Shoshone wife, Sacagawea, they hired the two to travel with them on the rest of their journey. Although neither explorer liked the rough, hot-tempered Charbonneau, they found Sacagawea a pleasant and valuable addition to the party.

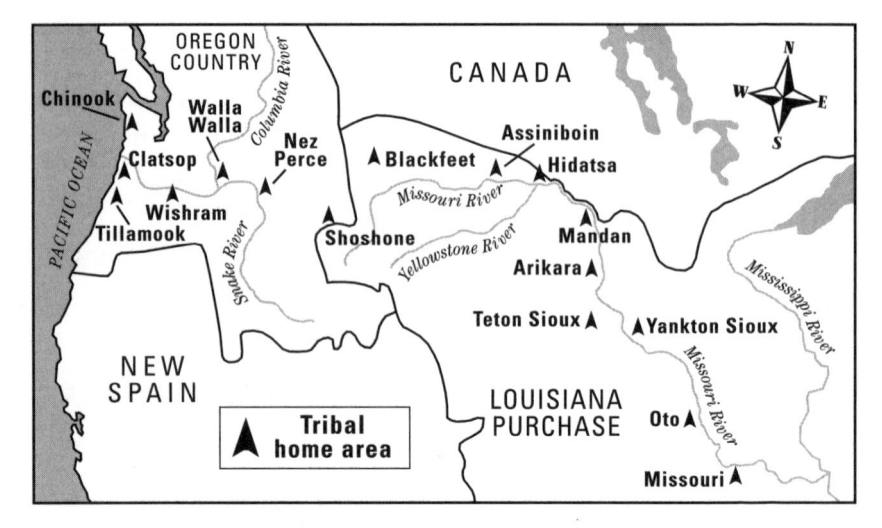

This map shows the home areas of some of the Native American peoples that the team met on its 1804-1806 journey.

On April 7, 1805, Lewis, Clark, and their new guides left Fort Mandan. With her two-month-old son strapped to her back, Sacagawea helped the explorers any way she could, including finding plants that were safe to eat.

One day in May, a sudden storm almost tipped over Charbonneau's boat. Lewis and Clark watched helplessly from shore as many of their supplies began to float away. Only Sacagawea stayed calm. She bravely sat in the boat and grabbed objects as they floated past. Her quick thinking saved many valuable objects, including the group's medicines and journals of their trip.

◆ Sacagawea ◆

In August 1805, Lewis and Clark met a large band of Shoshone near the border of Montana and Idaho. The Shoshone were about to attack. Suddenly, Sacagawea ran forward, yelling and dancing with delight. She had recognized the band's chief as her brother, Cameahwait. They had not seen one another since she was kidnapped. Cameahwait and the other Shoshone were thrilled to see Sacagawea again. They served as protectors to the explorers and later sold horses to them so they could complete their journey to the Pacific Ocean.

What Happened to Her?

In November 1805, Lewis and Clark and their team reached the Pacific Ocean. They spent the winter in Oregon. On March 23, 1806, they began the long

TOPICAL TIDBIT

Meeting the Natives

Lewis and Clark's team met nearly 50 different tribes of Native Americans on their journey west. Some tribes had never seen a white man before. The explorers developed a plan for explaining their situation to each group. They explained that the tribe had a new "great father," President Thomas Jefferson, back in the east. Then they gave the Indians gifts and performed a kind of parade, marching in their uniforms and shooting their guns. Sacagawea was important in helping to establish communication between the explorers and the Native Americans they met.

Gold-colored dollar coins, first issued in 2000, honor Sacagawea's place in American history.

journey home. Once again, Sacagawea, Charbonneau, and Pompey traveled with them. Sacagawea proved to be a great help guiding them back through the mountain passes. In his journal, William Clark called Sacagawea "the Indian woman, who has been of great service to me as a pilot through this country."

Sacagawea

LIFE EVENTS

About 1787
Sacagawea is born in what is now Idaho.

About 1800
Sacagawea is kidnapped and sold to another Indian tribe, then to a French fur trapper.

1804
Meriwether Lewis and William Clark start their expedition from St. Louis, Missouri.

1805
Sacagawea meets Lewis and Clark in what is now North Dakota. She, her husband, and baby son accompany the expedition. The team returns in 1806.

2000
The U.S. Mint issues new one-dollar coins honoring Sacagawea, with a picture of her on the face.

When the explorers reached North Dakota, Sacagawea, her husband, and son remained there while Lewis, Clark, and the rest of their team traveled on to Missouri. No one is sure what happened to Sacagawea after that. Some historians think that she died in 1812. But years later, a very old woman living on a Shoshone reservation in Wyoming claimed to be Sacagawea. She knew many details about Lewis and Clark, and so many historians believe her story. That woman died in 1884 and was buried on the reservation. A stone monument marks her grave, honoring her as "a guide with the Lewis and Clark expedition."

Whatever happened to Sacagawea, she has become much more than a mere guide. Her story of heroism and courage lives on in American history.

Robert Smalls
An Unlikely Hero
(born 1839 • died 1915)

Robert Smalls started life as a slave. Then a daring decision gave him his freedom and changed his life forever.

Life as a Slave

Robert Smalls was born in Beaufort, South Carolina, in 1839. His parents were slaves, so Robert began his life as a slave, too. Little is known about his childhood. It probably was spent working on his master's property in Beaufort.

When Robert was 12 years old, his owner hired him out to work in the shipyards of Charleston, South Carolina. There, Robert learned how to navigate ships—a skill that later proved very useful.

When the Civil War broke out in 1861, Smalls was 23 years old. He had a job driving a steam-powered ship named the *Planter*. In 1862, the *Planter* became part of the Confederate Navy. The ship was armed with four cannons and plenty of ammunition.

After Robert Smalls escaped from slavery, he went on to become a Civil War hero and a member of the U.S. House of Representatives.

A Daring Escape

On May 12, 1862, the *Planter*'s white captain and white crew went ashore for the evening. At 3 o'clock the next morning, Smalls, his wife and two children, and the 12 slave crewmen and their families took over the ship. They sailed it out of the harbor. In the dark,

◇ Courage ◇

Smalls was able to fool the watchmen: He pretended that he was the captain by wearing the captain's hat and imitating the way he walked. Smalls knew the signals, so he was able to sail past the Southern forces keeping guard. Then he ran up a white flag of surrender and delivered the ship to the Union Navy. "I thought the *Planter* might be of some use to Uncle Abe," he said, referring to President Lincoln.

The Union was pleased to get the *Planter* with its cannons and ammunition. Even more important was Smalls's knowledge about Confederate defenses and the tricky waters of Charleston Harbor. The U.S. government appointed Smalls as pilot of the *Planter* and sent the ship into service as a gunboat.

> "My race needs no special defense, for the past history of them in this country proves them to be the equal of any people anywhere. All they need is an equal chance in the battle of life."
> —Robert Smalls

On December 1, 1863, the *Planter* was caught by heavy fire from enemy guns. The captain panicked and abandoned the ship. Smalls courageously took command. He returned fire, then sailed the ship to safety. For his heroic actions, Robert Smalls was named captain of the ship. He remained captain until 1866, after the war.

Robert Smalls

A New Life

After the war, Smalls returned to Beaufort. He bought his former master's home, and soon became one of the city's most respected citizens. He also served in the state militia until 1877.

In 1868, Smalls entered politics. For a short time after the Civil War, African Americans were allowed to vote and hold office in the South. Smalls was elected as a delegate to South Carolina's constitutional convention, where he drafted a resolution for the state's first free educational system. Also in

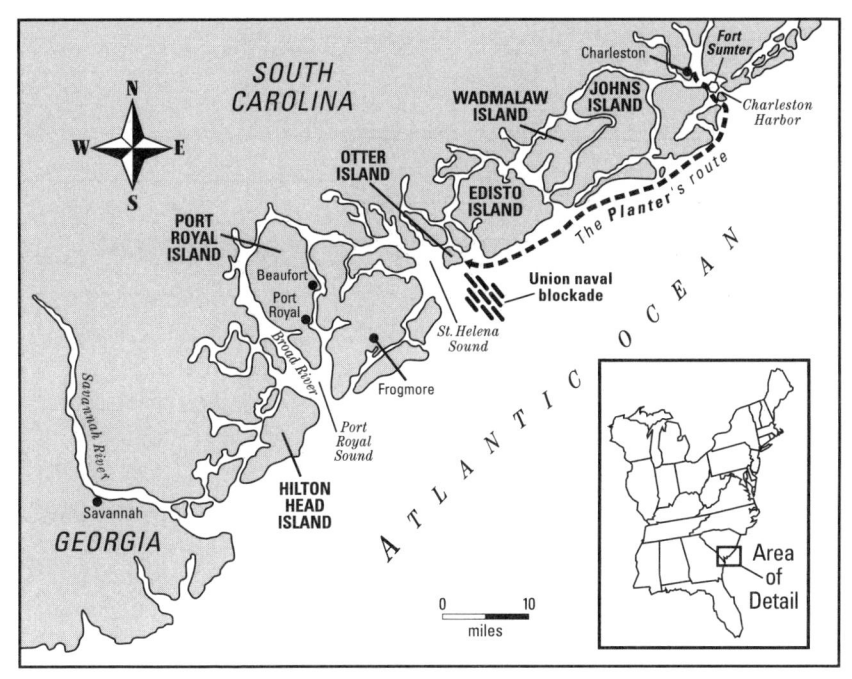

The dotted line shows the route that Robert Smalls took to freedom, sailing the Planter *out of Charleston Harbor on May 13, 1862.*

◇ Courage ◇

1868, he was elected to the South Carolina legislature. Two years later, he became a state senator.

In 1875, Smalls was elected to the U.S. House of Representatives. During his five terms, he introduced or supported several pieces of civil-rights law. Those bills gave former slaves the right to own property, sign contracts, and receive equal protection under the law.

Smalls left Congress in 1887. He remained active in politics. In 1895, he was one of six black delegates to South Carolina's state constitutional convention. There he tried, unsuccessfully, to pass laws to assure voting rights for black citizens.

TOPICAL TIDBIT

Black Americans Go to Washington

After the Civil War ended in 1865, the U.S. government tried to reform laws and customs in the South. This period is called Reconstruction, which means "rebuilding." During Reconstruction, Southern states began sending black politicians to Washington for the first time. The first African American representative in the U.S. House was Jefferson F. Long of Georgia, in 1869. Hiram Rhoades Revels was elected to fill the Mississippi Senate seat of Jefferson Davis, who had been president of the Confederate states. Revels was followed by Blanche K. Bruce, an ex-slave who had gone to Oberlin College. In all, 22 blacks were elected from Southern states.

◆ Robert Smalls ◆

A Hero Until the End

Smalls spent the last years of his life working with children at Beaufort's black school. He died in February 1915. Late in life, Smalls saw many rights taken away from African Americans as unfair laws were passed throughout the South. But he always believed that the U.S. would one day live up to its ideals of "life, liberty, and the pursuit of happiness" for all its citizens. ◆

LIFE EVENTS

1839
Robert Smalls is born in Beaufort, South Carolina.

1862
Smalls sails the Confederate ship *Planter* out of Charleston Harbor.

1863
Smalls is made captain of the *Planter*.

1875
Smalls is elected to the U.S. House of Representatives.

1895
Smalls is a delegate at South Carolina's state constitutional convention.

1915
Robert Smalls dies.

Mary Edwards Walker
Army Doctor
(born 1832 • died 1919)

Only recently have women been accepted into the armed forces and given the same opportunities as men. During the Civil War, however, Mary Edwards Walker served on battlefields and became the first woman ever to earn a Congressional Medal of Honor.

Strong Opinions

Mary Edwards Walker was born in Oswego, New York, on November 26, 1832. Her father was a doctor who believed strongly in education and equality for women. Following his example, Mary grew up believing in women's rights. She also became a follower of Amelia Bloomer, who called for more comfortable and practical clothes for women. As an adult, Mary Edwards Walker followed Bloomer's example of wearing loose-fitting pants (which became known as "bloomers") instead of the tight-fitting, bulky, and uncomfortable dresses women were expected to wear.

Mary Edwards Walker refused to be held back by society's unfair expectations for women.

In 1855, Walker graduated from Syracuse Medical College. She was the only woman in her class and only the second woman to graduate from a U.S. medical school. The following year, she married

Courage

another doctor, Albert Miller. Walker broke with tradition by keeping her own name instead of taking her husband's. The couple set up a medical practice together, but the business failed because most people would not accept a female doctor. Walker and Miller separated several years later, and were divorced in 1869.

On the Battlefield

In 1861, the U.S. Civil War broke out between the North and South. Walker traveled to Washington, D.C., and tried to join the Union Army. When she was refused a commission as a medical officer, Walker volunteered as an acting assistant surgeon at the U.S. Patent Office Hospital in Washington. She was the first female surgeon in the United States Army.

In 1863, General George H. Thomas appointed Walker assistant surgeon in the Army of the Cumberland. This finally placed her on the battlefield. Walker bravely served near the front lines for almost two years. She cared for hundreds of sick, injured, and dying soldiers, despite shortages of medicines and supplies. She also served as a spy, and crossed Confederate lines to treat civilians.

Walker was captured by Confederate forces in 1864. She spent four months in a prison in Richmond, Virginia, before being exchanged for a Confederate officer held prisoner by the Union army. Between her release and the war's end in April 1865, Walker worked at a prison for women in Louisville, Kentucky.

The Medal of Honor

On November 11, 1865, President Andrew Johnson awarded the Congressional Medal of Honor to Walker for her contributions to the war effort. She was the first woman to ever receive the Medal, which is the country's highest military award.

After the war ended, Walker was elected president of the National Dress Reform Association. The group campaigned for more comfortable and sensible

TOPICAL TIDBIT

Walt Whitman

One of the most famous volunteers of the Civil War is also one of America's greatest poets—Walt Whitman. When his brother George was wounded in the Battle of Fredericksburg, Virginia, in December 1862, Whitman rushed from his home in Brooklyn, New York, to the field hospital. After George recovered, Whitman took a job in nearby Washington, D.C. In his spare time, he volunteered his services to the wounded soldiers in the Army hospital. He read to the men, wrote letters for them, and spent what little money he had on small comforts for them. The poet stayed in Washington through the end of the war.

◆ Courage ◆

clothes for women. She often dressed as a man, including a top hat, bow tie, and long coat. Several times, she was arrested for disguising herself as a man, a charge that she found ridiculous.

Meanwhile, Walker's war work was publicized by several women's rights organizations. She became a hero to feminists. Walker worked for a variety of social reforms, including the campaign for women's right to vote. Walker attended political meetings and conventions, although she wasn't always allowed to speak because she was a woman. She also wrote several books.

In 1917, Walker received stunning news. Congress had changed the rules for awarding the Medal of Honor. They would now recognize only people who had been in "actual combat with an enemy." Walker, along with 910 other people, was asked to return her medal. Walker refused to return hers, and she continued to wear it every day until her death. In 1977, President Jimmy Carter reinstated her medal, praising Walker's patriotism, dedication, and loyalty to her country, even though

> "Dr. Mary lost the medal simply because she was a hundred years ahead of her time."
> —a relative of Mary Edwards Walker, to *The New York Times*

Mary Edwards Walker

LIFE EVENTS
1832   Mary Edwards Walker is born in Oswego, New York.
1855   Walker graduates from Syracuse Medical College—the second woman to graduate from a U.S. medical school.
1861   The Civil War begins. Walker volunteers and becomes the first female surgeon in the U.S. Army.
1864   Confederate forces capture Walker and hold her prisoner for four months.
1865   Walker is awarded the Congressional Medal of Honor.
1919   Mary Edwards Walker dies.

she was treated unfairly because of her sex.

Dr. Mary Edwards Walker died in Oswego, New York, on February 21, 1919. She died just a few months before women were finally awarded the right to vote. In 1982, the U.S. issued a stamp to honor Walker as the first woman to be awarded the Congressional Medal of Honor.

Ida B. Wells-Barnett
Antilynching Activist
(born 1862 • died 1931)

Ida B. Wells-Barnett saw terrible tension between whites and blacks in Mississippi after the Civil War. African Americans had just been freed from slavery, and many Southern whites resented them. Wells-Barnett was discriminated against not only because of her race, but also because of her gender. She devoted her life to improving the treatment of African Americans and women in the U.S.

Always a Fighter

Ida Bell Wells was born during the Civil War, on July 16, 1862, in Holly Springs, Mississippi. She had to be tough. Her parents were slaves who were freed after the war ended in 1865. Times were difficult for blacks in the South as they tried to adjust to life as free men and women. Most slave owners had denied slaves any schooling, so many former slaves could not read or write. It was hard to start businesses or farms on their own

Ida B. Wells-Barnett used her writing skills to call for equal treatment of all people.

◆ Courage ◆

because they had little money. They had worked for years as slaves, and received no payment.

Ida had the opportunity to go to school. She was very bright, and became a teacher herself at age 16, after her parents died. In 1884, she traveled to Tennessee to teach at a country school while attending Fisk University. In Tennessee, Ida experienced prejudice firsthand.

> "I felt that one had better die fighting against injustice than to die like a dog or rat in a trap."
> —Ida B. Wells-Barnett

One incident occurred in the mid 1880s, when she was thrown off a train for sitting in the whites-only section. The train had separate seating for white passengers and black travelers, but Ida refused to change seats when asked. She sued the railroad because it had not provided equal facilities. She won the case in local court and was awarded $500. Later, however, the Tennessee Supreme Court reversed the decision.

A Target of Hate

Ida B. Wells continued to stand up to injustice. She wrote articles about the poor quality of black schools, especially when compared to white schools, which were far superior. Wells lost her teaching job because of these articles so, in the late 1880s, she

◈ Ida B. Wells-Barnett ◈

began writing for a newspaper called the *Memphis Free Speech*. In her articles, she called for an end to discrimination and violence against blacks.

Wells spoke out most passionately against lynching, which was occurring throughout the South. Lynching was when angry mobs of white men hunted African American men and women and dragged them from their homes or jobs. The mobs would beat their victims, then hang them—often for no reason other than the color of their skin. The police, who were white, often ignored the murders.

Several of Wells's friends were lynched in the early 1890s. Her newspaper instructed blacks to boycott (refuse to use) white businesses in protest. She became a target herself, and her office was destroyed. Wells was warned to stay away or be killed.

TOPICAL TIDBIT

The Origins of Lynching

Lynching became popular in the U.S. during the American Revolution, under the direction of Charles Lynch, a planter and patriot from Virginia. He led a group that punished people who remained loyal to Great Britain. The practice became known as *lynching*, and continued for more than 150 years. Between 1882 and 1951, more than 1,290 whites and more than 3,400 blacks were lynched in the U.S.

◆ Courage ◆

Wells moved to New York and continued her work. In 1895, she married Ferdinand Lee Barnett. Wells kept her maiden name as part of her married name, and became Ida Wells-Barnett. Although this is relatively common today, it was rare, even shocking, in 1895. Also in 1895, Wells-Barnett published a book about lynching called *A Red Record*. Three years later, she urged President William McKinley to take government action to end lynching.

A Nonstop Activist

Wells-Barnett's fight did not end with African American issues. She also fought for women's rights. Wells-Barnett was proof that a woman could be a journalist, activist, wife, and mother of four children. She tried to combine race and gender

LIFE EVENTS

1862
Ida Bell Wells is born a slave in Holly Springs, Mississippi.

Mid 1880s
Wells is forced to sit in third class on a train, even though she had bought a first-class ticket. She sues the train company.

1891
Wells establishes the newspaper *Memphis Free Speech*. She writes articles that call for an end to violence against blacks.

1895
Ida B. Wells marries Ferdinand Lee Barnett and moves to Chicago.

1931
Ida B. Wells-Barnett dies.

Ida B. Wells-Barnett

issues, but some leaders of the women's movement were not very supportive. They feared that adding race to the mix would take interest and support from the women's movement.

Wells-Barnett started many groups to address social causes, including the Negro Fellowship League and the Alpha Suffrage Club. She was one of the founders of the National Association for the Advancement of Colored People (NAACP) in 1909. The NAACP is an organization that works toward establishing equal rights for African Americans. Wells-Barnett died on March 25, 1931, in Chicago, Illinois.

Ida B. Wells-Barnett described her struggles in her autobiography, *Crusade for Justice*. Although lynching continued into the 20th century, Wells-Barnett fought courageously in the face of death threats. She brought the issue before the eyes of the world and encouraged others to work toward ending injustice.

Chuck Yeager
Breaking the Sound Barrier
(born 1923)

In 1947, pilot Chuck Yeager *(YAY-gur)* did something that many people thought was not only dangerous, but physically impossible: He flew a plane faster than the speed of sound.

A Loner

Charles Elwood Yeager was born near Myra, West Virginia, on February 13, 1923. When he was four, his family moved to the nearby town of Hamlin. Chuck was good at math, but not very interested in school. He preferred to be out in the woods, exploring, hunting, or fishing. The boy was well liked, but had a reputation for being a loner who did things his own way.

Chuck's father owned a drilling business, and Chuck was fascinated by the machinery. He also enjoyed working on cars. After he graduated from high school in 1941, several people suggested that Chuck join the Army. After an Army official told him that he could be a pilot, Chuck was ready to go.

Chuck Yeager with the Bell X-1, nicknamed Glamorous Glennis, *the first airplane to break the sound barrier*

Earning His Wings

Chuck Yeager was studying aircraft mechanics in California on December 7, 1941, when the Japanese bombed Pearl Harbor. That attack prompted the U.S. to join World War II. Yeager was eager to learn how to fly in combat. Even though he became airsick during his first few flights, he soon earned his pilot's wings. On March 10, 1943, Yeager was named

◇ Courage ◇

a flight officer. By 1944, he was stationed in England and flying in combat missions over Europe.

During the war, Yeager flew 64 missions and shot down 13 German planes. His most frightening moment came on March 5, 1944, when he was shot down over German-occupied France. Yeager made his way across the border into Spain and, finally, back to his unit in England. During the journey, he and a companion were almost captured by German soldiers. Yeager's companion was seriously injured. Yeager saved the man's life and received the Bronze Star for his bravery and "complete disregard for his personal safety."

When the war ended in 1945, the Army assigned Yeager to be a flight instructor at an airfield in Texas. For Yeager, this job was boring after the excitement of combat flying. Later that year, Yeager became a test pilot at Wright Air Field in Dayton, Ohio. His job was to check out planes after they had been repaired and to inspect new planes being put into service.

The Mysterious Sound Barrier

By the mid-1940s, pilots could fly faster than ever before. However, something unusual happened when pilots flew very fast. The plane would shake and rock, and the controls would go wild. Some

Chuck Yeager

pilots couldn't control their planes, and were killed in crashes. The problem was something called the sound barrier.

> **"Somehow I always managed to live to fly another day."**
> —Chuck Yeager

When planes fly, they push waves of air in front of them. As they approach the speed of sound, called Mach 1 (about 760 miles per hour), the air in front of the planes has less time to move out of the way. This creates something like a wall of air that must be pushed through, which puts dangerous strains on the plane. At the time, many people believed that if a plane ever actually did reach Mach 1, it would crash into the built-up waves of air and be destroyed.

There was only one way to find out what might happen if a pilot flew faster than the speed of sound: Do it. A rocket-powered plane, called the Bell X-1, was designed to "break the sound barrier." Chuck Yeager was chosen to be the pilot of that plane. He named it the *Glamorous Glennis*, after his wife.

On October 14, 1947, a B-29 bomber towed the X-1 up to about 25,000 feet. Then Yeager, who was inside the X-1, released it from the B-29. His jet's rockets roared into life and Yeager zoomed up to 42,000 feet. He picked up speed, watching as the

◆ Courage ◆

indicator moved to 1.07 Mach—just past the speed of sound. Meanwhile, on the ground, scientists heard a distant bang. Yeager had safely broken the sound barrier—and caused the first sonic boom.

After the Flight

For security reasons, Yeager's remarkable achievement was kept secret for eight months. When the news was finally released, he became a national hero.

Yeager remained in the supersonic (faster than sound) flight program until 1954. He set several new records, including a world speed record of 1,650 miles per hour in 1953.

TOPICAL TIDBIT

The Right Stuff

Being a test pilot is a life of constant danger. In 1953, Chuck Yeager reached Mach 2.4 in his jet, only to spin out of control at 80,000 feet. He plunged 51,000 feet in 51 seconds (1,000 feet per second!) before regaining control. In 1963, Yeager again lost control and became the first pilot to eject himself from a jet in a pressurized suit used for high altitudes. The suit then caught fire from burning debris that was tangled up in the parachute. Yeager's coolness under pressure was the very definition of the kind of bravery that writer Tom Wolfe called *The Right Stuff*—a book which featured Yeager's story.

Retired general Chuck Yeager at a news conference at Edwards Air Force Base, California, on October 14, 1997.

◈ Courage ◈

By the time Chuck Yeager retired in 1975, he was a brigadier (one-star) general. He wrote an autobiography, *Yeager*, published in 1985, and was one of the subjects of *The Right Stuff*, a popular book and movie.

Chuck Yeager showed remarkable bravery in combat during World War II. He also had the courage to shatter a much-feared sound barrier—one that had killed people before him. His fearlessness is an awesome example of what a courageous person can accomplish. ◈

LIFE EVENTS

1923
Chuck Yeager is born in Myra, West Virginia.

1944
Fighter pilot Yeager is shot down over France during World War II.

1945
Yeager earns the title of "ace" with five confirmed "kills" of German aircraft in one day.

1947
Test pilot Yeager breaks the sound barrier in a Bell X-1 jet.

1976
President Gerald R. Ford awards Yeager the Congressional Medal for bravery.

1985
Yeager's autobiography, *Yeager*, is published.

Glossary and Pronunciation Guide

activist *(AK-tih-vist)* a person who believes in taking action to support a cause; p. 6

blockade *(blah-KAYD)* the use of barriers, such as troops or warships, to keep people or supplies from passing into or out of an area; p. 27

convention *(kun-VEN-shun)* a meeting of people or groups working toward a common purpose; p. 46

delegation *(del-uh-GAY-shun)* a group of people chosen to act or decide for others; p. 46

discrimination *(dis-krih-muh-NAY-shun)* different or unequal treatment; p. 6

expedition *(ek-spuh-DIH-shun)* a journey or trip taken for a specific purpose, such as exploring; p. 93

feminist *(FEH-muh-nist)* a person who believes in the equality of men and women; p. 110

frontier *(frun-TEER)* the area on the edge between the settled and unsettled part of a country; p. 13

gallant *(GA-lunt)* brave and honorable; p. 73

gender *(JEN-dur)* a grouping by sex, male or female; p. 112

heresy *(HER-uh-see)* believing or following an opinion that goes against the teachings of a religion or church; p. 68

humble *(HUM-bul)* modest; not luxurious; p. 47

Glossary and Pronunciation Guide

interpreter *(in-TUR-pruh-tur)* a person who translates from one language to another; *p. 93*

legislature *(LEH-jus-lay-chur)* an organized group that has the power to make laws; *p. 104*

lunar *(LOO-nur)* relating to the moon; *p. 12*

martyr *(MAR-tur)* a person who sacrifices his or her life for a belief or cause; *p. 65*

module *(MAH-jool)* part of a spacecraft that can be used as a separately operated unit; *p. 11*

navigate *(NA-vuh-gayt)* to steer a course in a ship or aircraft; *p. 100*

plantation *(plan-TAY-shun)* a large farm or other land area worked by laborers; *p. 42*

prejudice *(PREH-juh-dus)* a judgment or opinion formed without knowledge or fair cause; *p. 114*

register *(REH-juh-stur)* officially sign up, especially as a voter or student; *p. 42*

reservation *(reh-zur-VAY-shun)* an area of public land set aside for a specific use; *p. 34*

rites *(RYTES)* activities or acts that are part of a ceremony; *p. 34*

satellite *(SA-tuh-lyte)* an object that orbits Earth, the moon, or other bodies in space; *p. 10*

savage *(SA-vij)* a brutal, uncivilized person; *p. 31*

sonic boom *(SAH-nik boom)* a loud noise that occurs when the sound barrier is broken; *p. 122*

Index

A
Adams, John Quincy, 63
airplanes, 7, 22-23, 77, 78, 82, 83, 84, 85, 86, 118-124
The Alamo (San Antonio, Texas), 14, 16, 17
Aldrin, Edwin "Buzz", 11, 12
American Revolution, 6, 38, 40, 61, 64, 70-73, 74, 115
Apache Indians, 31-36
Armstrong, Neil, 5, 7-12
astronauts, 5, 7-8, 10-12, 87, 89, 91-92
astronomy, 8, 88

B
blockades, 27-28
Bowie, James, 13-17
Bowie knife, 14-15, 17
Bush, George W., 80

C
Catholicism and the Catholic Church, 65, 67, 68, 69
Challenger, 89, 90, 91, 92
Cherokee Indians, 70
civil rights, 6, 42, 45, 47, 104
Civil War, 25, 27-28, 29, 44, 50, 51, 52, 53, 101, 102, 103, 104, 106, 108, 109, 111, 112
Clark, William, 93, 95, 96, 97, 98, 99

D
The Dauphin—*see* Charles VII
Davis, Benjamin O., Jr., 18-24
Davis, Benjamin O., Sr., 18-19, 23
discrimination/prejudice, 6, 21, 23, 47, 111, 112, 114, 115

E
Eagle, 11, 12
Eastern Air Lines, 85, 86

F
Farragut, David, 25-30
French and Indian War, 40

G
Gemini space program, 8, 10, 11
Geronimo, 31-36
Goyathlay—*see* Geronimo
guerrilla warfare, 73

H
Hale, Nathan, 6, 37-41
Hamer, Fannie Lou, 42-47
works by, 47
Hickok, Wild Bill, 48-53
Hutchinson, Anne, 54-59
Hutchinson, William, 54, 56, 59

I
Indianapolis 500, 82
integration, 23, 24—*see also* segregation

J
Jackson, Andrew, 60-64
Jefferson, Thomas, 95, 97
Joan of Arc, 65-69

K
King, Martin Luther, Jr., 45
Korean War, 7, 24,

L
Lewis, Meriwether, 93, 94, 95, 96, 97, 99
Lincoln, Abraham, 102
Lynch, Charles, 115
lynching, 112, 115, 116, 117

M
Marion, Francis, 70-74
McAuliffe, Christa, 91
McCain, John, 75-80
Mississippi River, 28
Missouri River, 93
moon landing, 6, 7, 8, 10-12

N
NASA (*see* National Aeronautics and Space Administration)

N (continued)

National Aeronautics and Space Administration (NASA), 8, 10, 11, 12, 88, 89, 92
National Association for the Advancement of Colored People (NAACP), 117
New Orleans, Battle of, 62-63, 64

O

Orléans (France), Battle of, 67

P

physics, 8, 88, 92
pilots (plane), 7, 20, 22, 23, 75, 77, 78, 81, 82, 84, 118, 119, 120,121, 124— see also test pilots
Planter, 100, 101, 102, 103, 105

R

religious freedom, 54, 58
Rickenbacker, Eddie, 81-86
Ride, Sally, 87-92

S

Sacagawea, 93-99
satellites, 8, 91
Scott, David, 8
segregation, 20, 23—see also integration
Shoshone Indians, 93, 95, 97, 99
slavery, 48, 93, 100-101, 104, 112, 114, 116
Smalls, Robert, 100-105
sonic boom, 123
sound barrier, 118, 119 120, 121, 122, 124
space shuttles, 89, 90, 91, 92
Spanish-American War, 23
The Swamp Fox—see Marion, Francis

T

test pilots, 8, 11, 120, 122, 124
torpedoes, 25, 28, 29, 30
Tuskegee Airmen, 21-23, 24
Tuskegee Institute, 21

U

Underground Railroad, 48
U.S. Air Force, 23, 24, 84
U.S. Army, 18, 20, 23, 34, 35, 49, 50, 51, 53, 84, 111, 118, 120
U.S. Navy, 7, 8, 25, 27, 29, 30, 75, 79, 84, 102

V

Vietnam War, 24, 77-79, 80
voting, 42, 44-45, 46, 47, 103, 110, 111

W

Walker, Mary Edwards, 106-111
 works by, 111
War of 1812, 27, 62-63, 64
War with Mexico, 33
Washington, George, 39, 40
Wells-Barnett, Ida B., 6, 112-117
 works by, 116, 117
The White House, 63-64, 116
women's rights, 106, 110-112, 116
World War I, 81, 82, 83, 84, 86
World War II, 20, 24, 85, 86, 119, 120, 124

Y

Yeager, Chuck, 118-124